Amtlicher Führer Burgruine Henneberg
Ines Spazier
mit einem Beitrag von Doris Fischer

Burgruine Henneberg
in Südthüringen

STIFTUNG
THÜRINGER SCHLÖSSER
UND GÄRTEN

Titelbild: Burgruine Henneberg, Luftaufnahme
Umschlagrückseite: Blick vom Palas in die Rhön

Impressum

Redaktion Grit Heßland und Dr. Susanne Rott
Mitarbeit Bildredaktion Maria Porske
Lektorat Grit Heßland
Englische Übersetzung Anna Łukasiewicz-Tannhäuser
Satz und Bildbearbeitung Rüdiger Kern, Berlin
Druck und Bindung Grafisches Centrum Cuno, Calbe (Saale)
Bibliografische Information der Deutschen Nationalbibliothek
Die Deutsche Nationalbibliothek verzeichnet diese Publikation
in der Deutschen Nationalbibliografie; detaillierte bibliografische
Daten sind im Internet über http://dnb.dnb.de abrufbar.
Amtlicher Führer der Stiftung Thüringer Schlösser und Gärten
Erste Auflage 2023
© 2023 Stiftung Thüringer Schlösser und Gärten, Rudolstadt,
und Deutscher Kunstverlag GmbH Berlin München,
Lützowstraße 33, 10785 Berlin
ISBN 978-3-422-80172-1
www.deutscherkunstverlag.de

Inhaltsverzeichnis | Table of Contents

Lage und Forschungsgeschichte

Henneberg liegt circa zehn Kilometer südwestlich von Meiningen an der Straße von Würzburg nach Meiningen direkt an der Grenze zum Freistaat Bayern und damit an der Wasserscheide von Obermain und Werra (**Abb. 1**). Diese Straße, auch als Hohe Straße bezeichnet, ist ein alter Verkehrsweg zwischen Mitteldeutschland und Franken. Die Burg nimmt östlich des gleichnamigen Orts den so genannten Schlossberg ein, einen freistehenden Bergkegel aus Muschelkalkstein (**Abb. 2**). Mit 527 Meter über NN überragt er die umliegende Gegend um etwa 130 Meter.

Henneberg gehört historisch zur Siedlungslandschaft des Grabfeldes bzw. Grabfeldgaus, der sich aus Teilen des unterfränkischen Landkreises Rhön-Grabfeld und Teilen der Landkreise Schmalkalden-Meiningen und Hildburghausen zusammensetzt. Er umfasste ein Gebiet, das von der Fränkischen Saale im Süden bis zum oberen Mittellauf der Werra im Norden reichte. Im Westen wurde der Grabfeldgau von den Kuppen der hessisch-bayerischen Rhön und im Osten von den beiden Gleichbergen gerahmt. Henneberg liegt in seinem nördlichen Teil.

Die Befestigung befindet sich auf einem Nord-Süd ausgerichteten Bergsporn, der nach Süden flach ausläuft, sonst aber steil abfällt. Das Plateau wird vollständig von einer Ringmauer umgeben. Diese umschließt ein Areal von 120 (Nord-Süd) × 65 Metern (West-Ost), das sich nach Süden in seiner West-Ost-Ausdehnung auf 20 Meter einengt. Die gesamte Anlage ist von einem Graben-Wall-System umgeben und wird im Süden durch weitere zwei Gräben und Wälle verstärkt.

Seit 1845 wurden verschiedene Sicherungs- und Sanierungsarbeiten an der Burganlage vorgenommen. Ende des 19. Jahrhunderts grub der Landbaumeister Ernst Abesser zahlreiche Fundamente entlang der Ringmauer aus und verzeichnete sie in einem Lageplan (**Abb. 3**). Abesser entfernte dabei nur die oberen Erdschichten, bis er auf die ersten Fundamentreste stieß, das heißt, er legte vor allem die spätmittelalterlichen Befunde frei. Zum Glück für die nachfolgenden Forschergenerationen berührte er die urgeschichtlichen und hochmittelalterlichen Fundschichten des 10. bis 13. Jahrhunderts nicht.

Weitere Untersuchungen führte Friedrich Tenner, damaliger Leiter des Hennebergisch-Fränkischen Geschichtsvereins, im Jahr 1936 durch. Nach der Öffnung der innerdeutschen Grenze, in deren Sperrgebiet die Burgruine lag, fanden zwischen 1992 und 1995 im Nordwesten der Burg vier Ausgrabungskampagnen des Thüringischen Landesamts für Denkmal-

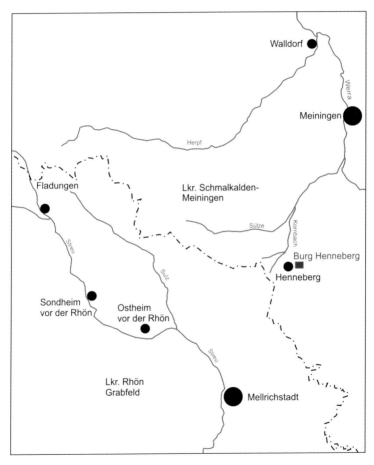

Abb. 1 | Fig. 1:
Lage der Burg Henneberg im Freistaat Thüringen
Location of Henneberg Castle in Thuringia

Abb. 2 | Fig. 2:
Blick auf die Burg Henneberg von Nordwesten
The north-west view of Henneberg Castle

Abb. 3 | Fig. 3:
Historischer Plan von
Ernst Abesser von
1880–1883
A 1880–1883 plan by
Ernst Abesser

pflege und Archäologie in Zusammenarbeit mit der Otto-Friedrich-Universität Bamberg und der Martin-Luther-Universität Halle-Wittenberg statt. Dabei wurde eine Fläche von ungefähr 750 Quadratmetern untersucht. 2001 erfolgten archäologische Untersuchungen im Bereich der südöstlichen Ringmauer, bei denen Reste eines bis dahin unbekannten mittelalterlichen Turms entdeckt wurden. Nach dem neusten Forschungsstand können fünf Bauphasen nachgewiesen werden: eine für das 7./6. Jahrhundert v. Chr., zwei für das Früh- bis Hochmittelalter und zwei für das Spätmittelalter (siehe Plan im hinteren Umschlag).

Geschichte der Henneberger Grafen und der Burg Henneberg

Die Ersterwähnung der Henneberger datiert in das Jahr 1096, als Gotebold II., Graf von Henneberg, einem Tauschgeschäft zwischen dem Hochstift Würzburg und dem unweit von Schwäbisch-Hall gelegenen Benediktinerkloster Comburg beiwohnte. Zu diesem Zeitpunkt existierte die Burg schon fast 100 Jahre. Sie wurde vermutlich im 10. Jahrhundert als Burg der Schweinfurter Grafen am nördlichen Randbereich ihrer Herrschaft gegründet. Die Schweinfurter, deren Herrschaftsraum an das südliche Grabfeld grenzte, förderten den Burgenbau im nördlichen Mainfranken. Sie hatten neben ihrem Stammgebiet auch Grundbesitz im Grabfeld. Es ist davon auszugehen, dass sie auch in den nördlich von Schweinfurt liegenden Randgebieten ihre Herrschaft durch ortsansässige Adlige stabilisieren wollten. Dazu können auch die späteren Grafen von Henneberg gehört haben. Als in der zweiten Hälfte des 10. Jahrhunderts die Burg Henneberg errichtet wurde, war das zu einem Zeitpunkt, als Graf Berthold von Schweinfurt und sein Sohn Heinrich ihre Machtpositionen gegenüber der Würzburger Kirche und dem Königtum stärken mussten.

Der Grundbesitz der Herrschaft baute sich auf den Besitztümern der Babenberger (Burg Bamberg, Franken) auf, von denen Poppo I., der erste nachweisbare Graf von Henneberg, abstammte. Ihre Reichslehen lagen im Thüringer Wald, von der Schleuse bis zur Hasel, sowie beim Schloss Lichtenberg nebst zugehörigem Umland. Außerdem hatten die Henneberger seit dem späten 11. Jahrhundert bzw. seit 1102 das Würzburger Burggrafenamt und die Würzburger Hochstiftsvogtei inne und mit diesen Reichsämtern Einfluss auf die Reichspolitik. Unter Gotebold II. (gest. 1144) wurde der Grundstein für die Bedeutung des Henneberger Grafenhauses gelegt. Er verschob den Schwerpunkt seiner Herrschaft nach Osten. In diesem Zusammenhang erfolgte 1131 die Gründung des Hausklosters in Veßra. Gotebold II. strebte einen geschlossenen Grundbesitz zwischen Schleusingen und Henneberg an. Damit geriet die Stammburg an den Rand des Herrschaftsgebiets.

Die Henneberger Grafen gewannen seit der zweiten Hälfte des 12. Jahrhunderts durch die Erbschaft der Herrschaft Nordeck (Zella-Mehlis, Thüringen) Einfluss nach Nordosten. Bis Mitte des 13. Jahrhunderts blieb der Besitz konstant. Das Grafenhaus teilte sich aber bereits 1190 in die Linien Henneberg sowie die Seitenlinien Botenlauben und Strauf. Die erste direkte urkundliche Erwähnung der Burg als „castrum" fällt in das Jahr 1221.

Unter Poppo VII. (gest. 1245), der mit Jutta, der Witwe des Meißener Markgrafen Dietrich der Bedrängte (gest. 1221), verheiratet war, begann eine kurze Blütezeit der Burg, die bis 1274 andauerte. Das 13. Jahrhundert wurde von einer regen Bautätigkeit auf der Burg begleitet, die archäologisch gut belegbar ist. Die Burg genügte nun den Ansprüchen Juttas, die aus dem Hause der Landgrafen von Thüringen stammte, als Wohnsitz. Dazu passt, dass 1253 in der Zeugenliste einer Urkunde Albrecht, Kaplan zu Henneberg, genannt wird. Daraus kann auf die Existenz einer Burgkapelle geschlossen werden, die sich auch archäologisch nachweisen ließ. Sie war einer Urkunde vom September 1464 zufolge der hl. Katharina geweiht.

Im Jahr 1246 trennte sich unter Hermann I. die Nebenlinie Coburg ab. Graf Heinrich III. (gest. 1262) hinterließ drei Söhne, die 1274 den Besitz aufteilten. Dadurch entstanden die Linien Schleusingen, Aschach und Hartenberg-Römhild. Die Henneburg fiel dabei an Berthold V. (gest. 1284), Begründer der Linie Henneberg-Schleusingen. Sein Sohn Berthold VII. (gest.

1340), der bedeutendste Vertreter des Grafenhauses, spielte in der Reichspolitik eine herausragende Rolle und war Ratgeber mehrerer Könige und
Kaiser. Unter seiner Herrschaft wurde Schleusingen zur Residenz ausgebaut
und die Burg Henneberg verlor ihre Bedeutung als Wohnsitz. Gleichzeitig
stieg aber ihr Wert als militärische Feste, da von ihr die Straße von Mellrichstadt nach Meiningen kontrolliert wurde. Beide Städte gehörten dem Würzburger Bischof. Im Zuge dieses Funktionswechsels kam es zu umfangreichen
Baumaßnahmen auf der Burg. Diese sprechen dafür, dass ein Bedeutungs-
verlust nicht unmittelbar spürbar wurde.

Im Mai 1393 gab Graf Heinrich X. von Henneberg-Schleusingen seine
Tochter dem Grafen Friedrich I. aus der Linie Römhild zur Ehefrau. Da er
die Mitgift von 4 000 Gulden nicht in barem Geld zahlen wollte oder konnte,
versetzte er dem Schwiegersohn eine Hälfte der Burg Henneberg bis zur
Auslösung durch Zahlung der Mitgift. Friedrich und seinen Erben stand die
Burg gegen jedermann offen, sie war also politisch und militärisch einsetz-
bar. Da die Mitgift nicht gezahlt wurde, kam es im April 1432 zur Aufteilung
der Burg unter den Söhnen Heinrichs und Friedrichs. Dies dürfte ihren Wert
als Wohnsitz und militärische Anlage deutlich gesenkt haben, da wichtige
Entscheidungen von nun an mit den Verwandten abzustimmen waren, die
nicht immer die gleichen territorialpolitischen Interessen hatten.

Während des Bauernkriegs wurde die Burg im Frühjahr 1525 verwüstet.
Die Einnahme durch schlecht bewaffnete Bauern zeigt, dass ihr militäri-
scher Wert damals nur noch gering war. Ein möglicher Wiederaufbau wurde
1527 kurz erwogen, aber nicht ausgeführt. Die Burg war allerdings bis zum
beginnenden 17. Jahrhundert noch teilweise bewohnt. Nach dem Erlöschen
der Linie Aschach fiel das Gebiet 1549 an die Linie Schleusingen. 1583 starb
diese mit Georg Ernst, Graf von Henneberg-Schleusingen, im Mannes-
stamm aus. Die Grafschaft samt Burgruine ging an die Wettiner, die sie aber
nur noch verwalteten.

Baugeschichte und archäologische Ausgrabungen

Die Burg Henneberg – eine Höhensiedlung des 7./6. Jahrhunderts v. Chr.

Der Burgberg wurde erstmals im 7./6. Jahrhundert v. Chr., in der so genannten Hallstattzeit, als Wohnsitz genutzt. Von dieser Höhensiedlung konnten zwei Gräben, zahlreiche in den Felsen eingetiefte Pfosten und eine Siedlungsschicht nachgewiesen werden. Aus den dokumentierten Pfosten ließen sich keine Hausgrundrisse rekonstruieren. Ein kleiner, bis 0,40 Meter tiefer Graben in der nordwestlichen Grabungsfläche war in den Kalkfelsen gehauen und diente der Aufnahme von Pfosten für eine Palisade oder für einen massiven Zaun (**Abb. 4**). Er wurde auf einer Länge von etwa 13 Metern dokumentiert und verlief bogenförmig über das nordwestliche Plateau. Der Graben folgte nicht unmittelbar der Hangkante oder dem Hang und wurde von zwei recht massiven Pfostengruben flankiert. Diese gehörten zu einer Pforte, die jedoch weniger als 0,80 Meter breit war und daher zweifelsohne nicht den primären Zugang zum Siedlungsareal bildete.

Eine weitere, aber gestörte Grabenstruktur befand sich in der südlichen Grabungsfläche. Sie verlief von Südosten nach Nordwesten, also annähernd quer über das Plateau. Mit einer Sohlbreite von circa 1,50 Metern und einer Tiefe von bis zu 0,70 Metern übertraf der Befund den Palisadengraben der Nordfläche erheblich. Der Graben war mit zahlreichen großen, plattigen Kalksteinen aufgefüllt worden. Er dürfte einen Befestigungscharakter besessen haben. In diesem Zusammenhang ist vermutlich auch das dem Burggraben im Süden vorgelagerte, dreifach gestaffelte Wall-Graben-System zu sehen. Dieses kann aber nicht sicher datiert werden.

Die hochmittelalterlichen Bauphasen

Ab Mitte des 10. Jahrhunderts wurde der Henneberger Schlossberg wieder systematisch zu einer Burganlage ausgebaut. Dies geschah etwa 100 Jahre, bevor die Henneberger erstmals in den urkundlichen Quellen auftraten. Von dieser hochmittelalterlichen Befestigung (10.–12. Jahrhundert) lagen vor Beginn der Ausgrabungen 1992 bis 1995 und 2001/02 keine Informationen vor. Auch die Untersuchungen von Ernst Abesser im 19. Jahrhundert und von Friedrich Tenner 1936 erbrachten zum hochmittelalterlichen Siedlungsgeschehen keine Aussagen.

Zwei hochmittelalterliche Bauphasen konnten in der nordwestlichen und in der südlichen Grabungsfläche erfasst werden. Der nordwestliche Bereich liegt auf dem höchsten Punkt des Plateaus. Zur ersten Bauphase gehörte ein circa 7,50 × 7,50 Meter großer Fachwerkbau (**1; Gebäude I**), der in der zweiten Hälfte des 10. Jahrhunderts auf der höchsten Stelle der Innenfläche errichtet worden war und durch einen Brand zerstört wurde. Direkt östlich schloss ein zweites Gebäude (**6; Gebäude II**) an, dessen unterste Fundamentbereiche sich als Mörtelauflagen auf einer Fläche von circa 9 × 3 Metern ausdehnten. Zwischen beiden Gebäuden lagen zwei Feuerstellen, die im frühen 11. Jahrhundert genutzt wurden.

In der Mitte des 11. Jahrhunderts setzte die zweite hochmittelalterliche Bauphase ein, die bis zum beginnenden 13. Jahrhundert dauerte. Unter Gotebold II. (gest. 1144) wurde nicht nur der Grundstein für das Henneberger Gra-

Abb. 4 | Fig. 4:
Ein Gräbchen sicherte im 7./6. Jahrhundert v. Chr. im Nordwesten der Burg einen Hofbereich
A ditch secured the inner area in the northwest of the castle in the 7–6th century BC

Abb. 5 | Fig. 5:
Im 12. Jahrhundert errichtete man Gebäude in Opus-spicatum-Bauweise
In the 12th century several buildings were erected in opus spicatum (herringbone pattern)

Abb. 6 | Fig. 6:
Das Gebäude III hatte eine Deckung aus Flachziegeln im Spitzschnitt
Building III was covered with pointed roof tiles and white glazed ridge tiles

Abb. 7 | Fig. 7:
Der herrschaftliche Wohnbereich im Nordwesten der Burg
View of the northern building complex

fenhaus mit den umfangreichen Besitzungen gelegt, sondern auch auf der Stammburg eine sehr rege Bautätigkeit entfaltet. Auf dem höchsten Punkt seines Wohnsitzes im Nordwesten der Burg entstand nach der Niederlegung des Gebäudes I ein 9 × 9 Meter großer Fachwerkbau (1; **Gebäude III**), der nach Süden einen Anbau hatte. Zu Beginn des 13. Jahrhunderts wurde der Bau wieder abgebrochen. Das Mauerwerk war in der fischgrätartigen Opus-Spicatum-Technik gesetzt und 0,90 Meter breit (**Abb. 5**). Zu dem Gebäude gehörten grüne Glasfenster. Es hatte eine Ziegeldeckung aus Flachziegeln im Spitzschnitt und weiß glasierte Firstziegel (**Abb. 6**), so wie auch der nach Süden anschließende, circa 10 × 10 Meter große **Wohnturm** (15; **Gebäude IV**). Dieser bestand aus Kleinsteinquadermauerwerk und wird mit einer Mauerstärke von circa 1,70 Metern ein vollständig steinernes Gebäude gewesen sein (**Abb. 7**).

Nördlich von Gebäude III lag ein weiteres Bauwerk (1; **Gebäude V**), das vor allem aus roten und hellgelben Buntsandsteinen bestand und sich auf einer Innenfläche von circa 4,30 × 3,50 Metern ausdehnte. Naturwissenschaftliche Untersuchungen datieren seine Entstehung in die Zeit um circa 1100

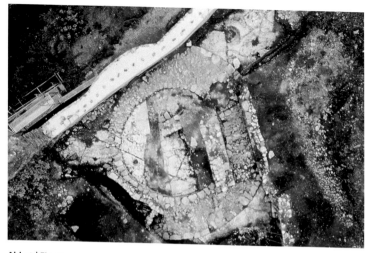

Abb. 8 | Fig. 8:
Der Rundturm (Bergfried I) aus dem 11. Jahrhundert (Aufnahme 2002)
The round tower (Tower I), constructed in the 11th century (photo 2002)

und damit in die Regierungszeit Gotebolds II. Unmittelbar nach Nordosten folgte ein fast quadratischer Bau (3,80 × 3 Meter), der mit einer Innenfläche von 2,40 × 2 Metern ein kleiner Turm war, vielleicht mit einem auskragenden Fachwerkobergeschoss (2; **Gebäude VI**). Der im Norden liegende **Brunnen** (4) entstand vermutlich ebenfalls im Hochmittelalter.

Im 11. Jahrhundert war auch der Südteil der Burganlage bebaut. Aus der Zeit um 1000/30 stammt ein in Schalenmauertechnik gesetzter Rundturm (19; **Bergfried I**), dessen Fundamente bei den Ausgrabungen freigelegt werden konnten und der als ältester mittelalterlicher Rundturm Thüringens gilt. Er hatte einen Außendurchmesser von 11,70 Metern bei einer Mauerstärke von 2,70 Metern (**Abb. 8**). An den Turm schloss zeitgleich eine 0,70 Meter breite Mauer an, die auf einer Länge von 3,40 Metern nachgewiesen wurde und als älteste Ringmauer gedeutet werden kann. Dieser Befund lässt erahnen, dass die gesamte Burg bereits im Hochmittelalter mit einer Ringmauer befestigt war. Höchstwahrscheinlich lag beim Rundturm das **erste Burgtor** (20). Dafür spricht vor allem die Topografie des Geländes mit dem allmählichen Anstieg zur Burg aus Südwesten im Gegensatz zu dem steileren, ab dem Spätmittelalter genutzten Westanstieg. Den südlichen Zugang sicherte man zusätzlich mit einem doppelten **Wall-Graben-System**, das bereits im 7./6. Jahrhundert v. Chr. entstanden sein könnte.

Der Rundturm wurde spätestens Ende des 12. bzw. zu Beginn des 13. Jahrhunderts abgerissen. Es stellt sich die Frage, warum ein so mächtiger Burgturm nur circa 150 Jahre existiert haben soll. Vermutlich um 1200 kam es zum Abbruch der Felskante und damit auch zum Abrutschen der ersten Befestigungsmauer. Somit stand der Turm nun direkt an der Felskante und wurde aus diesem Grund aufgegeben und abgetragen. Das freigelegte Turmfundament blieb bei der Sanierung der Ringmauer 2002 erhalten. Es wurde im Boden belassen und mit Vlies abgedeckt.

Interessant ist der Vergleich mit Burgtürmen, die vor allem im 12. Jahrhundert unter den Henneberger Grafen errichtet worden sind. Nach Vorgabe der Henneberger Stammburg (Außendurchmesser 11,70 Meter) entstanden im 12. bzw. frühen 13. Jahrhundert die Burgtürme in Botenlauben, Lkr. Bad Kissingen (Nordturm, Außendurchmesser 11,20 Meter), auf der Burg Nordeck bei Stadtsteinach, Lkr. Kulmbach (Außendurchmesser circa 11 Meter) und in Dillstädt, Lkr. Schmalkalden-Meiningen (Außendurchmesser circa 10 Meter). Die Ähnlichkeit aller vier hennebergischen Burgtürme ist auffallend und sucht ihresgleichen im deutschsprachigen Raum.

Nach Abbruch des Rundturms wurde der Zugang zur Burg nach Nordwesten verlegt. Hier fallen im Grabungsplan zwei im stumpfen Winkel zueinander laufende Mauern mit einer Mauerstärke von 1,50 Metern und einer Länge von 2,70 Metern bzw. 2,20 Metern auf. Sie waren als Schalenmauerwerk mit einer Sichtmauer nach Westen ausgeführt. Der Mauerzug gehörte zu einem **Zangentor (3)** mit stark nach innen einziehenden Mauerenden, wie sie in karolingisch-ottonischer Zeit typisch für den Burgenbau waren. So entstand eine lang gestreckte Torgasse. Von diesem Tor konnten nur Teile der westlichen Torwange und dabei nur der eigentliche Zugangsbereich ergraben werden. Die beiden Torwangen, die die Torgasse bildeten, lagen außerhalb der heutigen Ringmauer auf einem Plateau, das im Spätmittelalter abgearbeitet wurde. Die nach Osten anschließende gesamte Torsituation war durch die Abesser'schen Abgrabungen im 19. Jahrhundert beseitigt worden. Bei elektromagnetischen Untersuchungen kam im Norden eine Mauer zum

Vorschein, die bogenförmig auf den nordwestlichen Plateaurand zulief. Sie traf dort auf das Zangentor. Noch heute tritt an dieser Stelle die Nordwand einer spätmittelalterlichen Kemenate aus der Flucht der Ringmauer heraus (siehe Abb. 29), so dass vermutet werden kann, dass hier ursprünglich ein zur hochmittelalterlichen Toranlage gehörender Turm stand. Der Fels zeichnet an dieser Stelle den bogenförmigen Verlauf der hochmittelalterlichen Ringmauer nach. Außerdem ist dort, wo das Zangentor lag, im Felsen eine deutliche Einsattelung zu erkennen.

Die Grundfläche der hochmittelalterlichen Burg war mit knapp 8 000 Quadratmetern ursprünglich wesentlich größer als die heutige Fläche von circa 5 000 Quadratmetern. Das Felsplateau ging allmählich und abflachend in die Böschung über. Es ist anzunehmen, dass der Böschungsrand entweder mit einer Trockenmauer, einem geschütteten Wall oder einer Kombination aus beidem befestigt war.

Die spätmittelalterlichen Bauphasen

Für das Spätmittelalter konnten ebenfalls zwei Bauphasen nachgewiesen werden. Sie datieren vom 13. bis Mitte des 14. Jahrhunderts sowie von der zweiten Hälfte des 14. bis zum Beginn des 16. Jahrhunderts.

Wohl im Zusammenhang mit der Heirat Poppos VII. mit Jutta errichtete man zu Beginn des 13. Jahrhunderts einen Wohnbau (1; **Palas I**) und legte dafür die hochmittelalterlichen Gebäude III, V und VI nieder. Er war circa 13,50 Meter lang und zwischen 7,70 Meter und 8,50 Meter breit. Im Norden wurde ein turmartiger Bau an das Gebäude angefügt. Der Fußboden im Inneren bestand aus Kalksteinmörtel und Buntsandsteinplatten. Das Gebäude stand ursprünglich frei, wie ein Eckverband aus Buntsandsteinquadern an der Außenseite erkennen lässt, und wurde bei der Errichtung der spätmittelalterlichen Ringmauer in diese integriert (**Abb. 9**). Wahrscheinlich unmittelbar nach dem Wohnbau (Palas) errichtete man einen kleinen **Rundturm (13)**, der einen Außendurchmesser von 8,70 Metern bei einer Mauerstärke von circa 1,30 Metern hatte.

Poppo VII. (gest. 1242) ließ vermutlich auch in den hochmittelalterlichen, 10 × 10 Meter großen Wohnturm (Gebäude IV) eine Kapelle einbauen. So entstand im 13. Jahrhundert ein **Kapellenturm (15)**. Ein Kaplan auf der Burg

Abb. 9 | Fig. 9:
Die Westwand des Palas ist in die Ringmauer integriert (Aufnahme 1990/91)
The western wall of the palas is integrated into the curtain wall (photo 1990/91)

wird bereits 1253 bezeugt. Im Osten des Kapellenturms wurde wahrscheinlich im 14. Jahrhundert ein 3/5-Chor mit zwei Öffnungen im Nordwesten und Nordosten angefügt (siehe Abb. 7).

Der Innenhof zum Palas war vom übrigen Burggelände durch eine **Toranlage (10)** abgeriegelt. Sie lag etwa neun bis zehn Meter östlich des Palas und wurde von zwei fast quadratischen, circa 2,90 × 2,50 Meter messenden Gebäuden gerahmt. Im fünf Meter breiten Zwischenraum befand sich das Tor. Zahlreiche Militaria-Funde wie Sporen, Hufeisen, Hufnägel und Tüllengeschossspitzen zeugen von Kampfhandlungen im 13. und 14. Jahrhundert in diesem Bereich (**Abb. 10**).

Ob der Bergfried im Norden (**18; Bergfried II**) noch unter Poppo VII. oder unter seinem Nachfolger Heinrich III. (gest. 1262) und dessen Söhnen errichtet wurde, ist bislang nicht geklärt. Nach neuesten bauhistorischen Untersuchungen wird seine Errichtung um 1250 vermutet. Mit einem Außendurchmesser von 14 Metern bei einer Mauerstärke von 3,40 Metern und einem Innendurchmesser von 7,20 Metern dominierte er die Burg. Erhalten

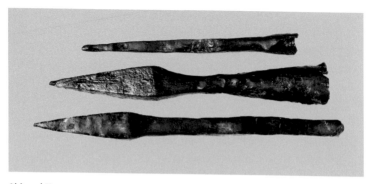

Abb. 10 | Fig. 10:
Zahlreiche Militariafunde wie diese Geschossspitzen wurden am Tor zum Wohnbau (Palas) gefunden
Numerous militaria finds were discovered near the gate to the residential building (palas)

hat sich sein Untergeschoss mit einer Höhe von circa 14 Metern. Er besteht aus roten und weißen Buntsandsteinquadern im unteren Bereich und im oberen aus Muschelkalksteinen **(Abb. 11)**.

Unter Berthold VII. (gest. 1340) verlagerte sich die Herrschaft nach Schleusingen. Die Henneburg verlor als Wohnsitz ihre Bedeutung und wurde mit umfangreichen Baumaßnahmen zur militärischen Festung umgestaltet. Es entstanden zahlreiche neue Gebäude. Südlich anschließend an den kleinen Rundturm im Nordwesten errichtete man ein unterkellertes Gebäude mit einer **Holzstube (14)** im Erdgeschoss (siehe Abb. 7). Sie war mit einer Innenfläche von 8,70 × 8,20 Metern fast quadratisch. Holzstuben stellen eine bauliche Besonderheit dar und kommen vor allem auf Burgen in Süddeutschland bzw. in Böhmen im Spätmittelalter vor.

Etwa in der Flucht zu den beiden quadratischen Bauten der Hoftoranlage entstand im 13. Jahrhundert ein weiterer Torturm mit den Maßen 6 × 6 Meter **(5; Gebäude VIII)**. Dies geschah nach dem Abbruch des Zangentors, von dem Teile beim Turmbau zweitverwendet wurden.

Für das Jahr 1308 ist in den schriftlichen Quellen ein Blitzschlag bezeugt, der einen Brand auslöste und zum Einsturz eines großen Turms führte. Brandrötungen des Felsens zwischen dem Rundturm beim Wohnbau (Palas) und dem Kapellenturm sprechen dafür, dass vielleicht sogar beide Türme einstürzten. Der Rundturm wurde daraufhin teilabgetragen, die Südwand des Wohnbaus verändert und der Unterbau des Turms in das Gebäude integriert. Der Kapellenturm bekam zur Stabilisierung im Nordwesten ein gleichschenkliges Mauerdreieck vorgeblendet. Durch die Verlängerung des einen Schenkels nach Nordosten und Hinzufügen einer von Nordwest nach Südost verlaufenden Mauer, die an das Fundament der ehemaligen Toreinfahrt grenzte, entstand ein trapezförmiges Gebäude (12; **Gebäude** IX) mit einem Eingang auf der Hofseite im Nordwesten (siehe Abb. 7). Die Grabungsergebnisse lassen auf einen Fachwerkbau schließen.

Das Südareal wurde im frühen 13. Jahrhundert als Bauplatz (21; **Steinbearbeitungsgrube**) – wahrscheinlich für die Errichtung des Palas – genutzt. Nach Aufgabe der Grube entstand dort Ende des 13. Jahrhunderts ein rechteckiges Gebäude (22; **Gebäude** X), von dem sich ein Gebäudetrakt von circa 6 × 5 Metern erhalten hat. Er wurde nach der archäologischen Untersuchung wieder zugeschüttet.

Abb. 11 | Fig. 11:
Der 15 m starke Turm (Bergfried II) aus der Mitte des 13. Jahrhunderts
The measuring 15 m in diameter tower (Tower II) from the middle of the 13th century

Abb. 12 | Fig. 12:
Das im Spätmittelalter verkleinerte Burgplateau mit der neuen Ringmauer und Resten der Zwingermauer im Nordosten (Blick von Westen)
In the Late Middle Ages the castle grounds were reduced in size and surrounded by a new curtain wall. Parts of the outer ward wall are still visible in the north-east (view from west)

Ende des 13. Jahrhunderts oder in der ersten Hälfte des 14. Jahrhunderts verkleinerte man das Burgplateau von 8 000 auf 5 000 Quadratmeter. Mit einem enormen Arbeitsaufwand wurde das Plateau senkrecht abgearbeitet und wiederum mit einer Ringmauer umgeben. Die im Nordwesten schon existierenden Gebäude Palas, kleiner Rundturm und wahrscheinlich auch die Holzstube standen nun direkt an der Plateaukante und wurden in die **neue Ringmauer** eingebunden (**Abb. 12**). Aus diesem Grund ragt der kleine Rundturm heute aus dieser heraus, während er ursprünglich auf dem damals viel breiteren Plateau errichtet worden war. Im Norden entstand vor der Burgmauer ein **Zwinger (7)** und in diesem Zusammenhang das **dritte Burgtor (16)** in der Nähe des heutigen Tors. Die noch in Teilen erhaltene Zwingermauer verlief am nördlichen Plateaurand parallel zur Ringmauer. Sie schloss im Osten an die Ringmauer an und endete im Westen beim Zwingertor, dem „äußeren Burgtor". Bei der Verkleinerung der Wohnfläche durch das senkrechte Abschlagen der Felswände entstand mittels Aufschüttung der abgebrochenen Steinmassen im Süden, Westen und Osten ein Wall-Graben-System, das im Norden bis zum Zwinger führte. Der an der Ostseite der Burg verlaufende Graben mit begleitendem Wall könnte bereits im Hochmittelalter angelegt worden sein.

Im Zusammenhang mit der Umgestaltung zur militärischen Feste im 14. Jahrhundert wurde die Burg zu ihrem Schutz mit bis zu 15 Burgmannen besetzt. So entstanden zahlreiche Burgmannensitze (**Kemenaten**) entlang der Ringmauer. Reste dieser Kemenaten haben sich im Norden erhalten (**8, 9**).

Im Verlauf des 15. Jahrhunderts fanden bis auf den Umbau des Wohnbaus (Palas I), die Errichtung des Brunnenhauses und den Umbau der Hoftoranlage keine großen Neubauarbeiten statt. Die Grabungsergebnisse belegen, dass im 15. Jahrhundert der erste, spätmittelalterliche Palas (Palas I) durch einen Brand teilzerstört und dessen Süd- und Ostwand umgestaltet wurde. Der neue Palas (**Palas II**) erhielt einen Arkadengang, der sich zum Hof hin öffnete. Drei Fundamente dieser Arkaden sind heute noch erhalten. Der im 13. Jahrhundert erbaute kleine Rundturm wurde teilweise abgebrochen und dessen Fundamentbereich in den Palas integriert und überwölbt, vermutlich als Küchentrakt. Der so entstandene Bau hatte eine Länge von circa 25 Metern und eine Breite von zehn bis elf Metern (Palas II). In einer Grafik aus

Abb. 13 | Fig. 13:
Walther, nach Wilhelm Adam Thierry, die Burgruine mit dem spätgotischen Wohnbau
von Norden, Aquatinta, um 1803
Walther, after Wilhelm Adam Thierry, the castle ruin with the late gothic residential
building, aquatint, 1803

dem Jahr 1803 sind die Arkaden mit der aufgelösten Hofwand des spätgotischen Palas sowie im Hintergrund das in den Wohnbau einbezogene Rundturmfragment zu sehen **(Abb. 13)**.

Südlich der heute noch erhaltenen Kemenate entstand ein weiteres, unterkellertes Gebäude, die **Kemenate der Familie von Trott (9)**. In diesem Zusammenhang wurde die **Hoftoranlage (11)** umgestaltet. Sie verlief nun vom Kapellenturm zur Südwestecke des Trott`schen Hauses. Der Anschlag des Torriegels ist dort immer noch erkennbar.

Ende des 15. und zu Beginn des 16. Jahrhunderts wurde die Ringmauer bis auf wenige Passagen im Nordwesten weitgehend erneuert, wobei man das heutige **Tor (17)** um 1500 in zwei ältere Ringmauerabschnitte einfügte und aus der Flucht nach innen versetzte.

Abb. 14 | Fig. 14:
Christian Juncker, Ansicht der Burg von Westen, kolorierte Federzeichnung, 1703
Christian Juncker, western view, pen and ink drawing, 1703

Nach der Verwüstung der Burg im Bauernkrieg 1525 erfolgten seit 1576 partielle Abrissarbeiten am Bergfried. Die Burg wurde aber teilweise noch bis zum beginnenden 17. Jahrhundert bewohnt. Danach fiel die Anlage wüst. 1784 ließ Herzog Georg I. von Sachsen-Meiningen (1761–1803) den Burghof planieren. Die erste detailreiche Aufnahme der Burgruine findet sich 1703 in dem ungedruckten Werk *Ehre der gefürsteten Grafschaft Henneberg* von Christian Juncker (**Abb. 14**). Sie zeigt zu Beginn des 18. Jahrhunderts die gesamte Burganlage von Westen. Im 19. Jahrhundert wurde neben der Darstellung der Gesamtansicht des Burgbergs vor allem das Innere der Burg mit den Ruinen des spätgotischen Wohnbaus in verschiedensten Grafiken abgebildet.

Die archäologischen Funde

Das Fundmaterial aus den Grabungen datiert in das 7./6. Jahrhundert v. Chr., in das Mittelalter und in die Neuzeit. Die urgeschichtlichen Inventare bestehen vor allem aus Keramikscherben (circa 5 300 Stück) und wenigen

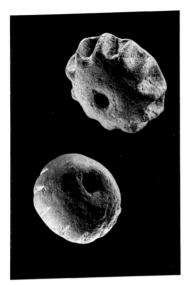

Abb. 15 | Fig. 15:
Zwei Spinnwirtel gehören zu den Funden
des 7./6. Jahrhunderts v. Chr.
Amongst the finds of the 7–6th century BC
there are two whirls

Abb. 16 | Fig. 16:
Die Bernsteinperle aus der Mitte des
6. Jahrhunderts v. Chr. kam wohl als Import
auf die Burg
The amber bead, dating to the middle
of the 6th century BC, was most likely an
import

Kleinfunden. Dazu zählen unter anderem ein Trichter und zwei Spinnwirtel
aus gebranntem Ton (**Abb. 15**) sowie ein Armring, zwei Tüllen und ein Beil aus
Bronze. Bemerkenswert ist eine gut erhaltene, gedrechselte Bernsteinperle
(**Abb. 16**), die wahrscheinlich als Import nach Henneberg gekommen ist.

Unter den über 16 400 geborgenen mittelalterlichen Keramikscherben
sind besonders Stücke mit frühen Bleiglasuren erwähnenswert. Sie datieren in das 11. bis frühe 13. Jahrhundert. Weiterhin bemerkenswert ist eine
rote Drehscheibenware, die mit höchster Wahrscheinlichkeit im späten 12.
bis frühen 13. Jahrhundert in Mayen, Lkr. Koblenz-Mayen, gefertigt wurde.
Henneberg ist nach gegenwärtigem Forschungsstand der südöstlichste Ver-
breitungspunkt dieser Keramik. Im späten 12. bis frühen 14. Jahrhundert be-
nutzte man auf der Burg auch Gefäße, die aus einem groben weißen Ton

Abb. 17 | Fig. 17:
Ein Gefäßboden mit aufwendiger
Verzierung
A bottom of a pot with an elaborate
decoration

Abb. 18 | Fig. 18:
Eiserne Maultrommeln sind selten. Meist
fertigte man sie aus Bronze
Iron jaw harps are relatively rare. They were
usually made of copper alloy

hergestellt worden sind. Dazu gehört ein Gefäßboden mit einer aufwendigen rotbraunen Bemalung (**Abb. 17**).

Kleinere mittelalterliche Tonobjekte sind Teile von Kleinplastiken, Spielsteine, Murmeln, Spinnwirtel und Webgewichte. Gefunden wurden Werkzeuge wie Messer, Scheren, Bohrer, Sicheln, eine Feile, eine Axt und eine Hacke. Teile von Schlosskästen, Schlüssel, Türangeln, Nägel, Bolzen, Haken und Beschläge, aber auch ein Kerzenständer stammen aus dem häuslichen Umfeld. Geschossspitzen kommen in einer großen Typenzahl vor. Trensen, Sporen, ein Steigbügel, ein Pferdestriegel, Sattelgurtschnallen, Hufeisen und Hufnägel zählen zum Pferdezubehör. Ein besonderer Fund ist eine eiserne

Abb. 19 | Fig. 19:
Der Ohrring datiert in das 12. Jahrhundert,
der kleine Ring in das 13. Jahrhundert
The earring dates from the 12th century, the
small ring from the 13th

Abb. 20 | Fig. 20:
Ein rhombischer Messingbeschlag aus dem
Frühmittelalter
An early medieval rhombic brass fitting

Abb. 21 | Fig. 21:
Der Ring gehörte dem Burgmann Mathes
von Hönningen, der 1576 verstarb
The ring belonged to Mathes von Hönnin-
gen, who was one of the Burgmannen of
Henneburg and died in 1576

Abb. 22 | Fig. 22:
Vergoldeter Bronzeanhänger aus dem
frühen 13. Jahrhundert mit einer Henne,
dem Wappentier der Henneberger Grafen
A gilded bronze pendant depicting a hen,
the heraldic animal of the Henneberg
family (13th century)

Maultrommel aus dem 12. Jahrhundert **(Abb. 18)**. Aus Buntmetall gearbeitet
wurden Finger- und Ohrringe, Ketten, Anhänger, Schließen, Knöpfe und
neuzeitliche Münzen **(Abb. 19)**. Mittelalterliche Münzen sind nicht überliefert. Um 1832 soll jedoch Johann Philipp Heinrich Hartmann bei ersten Son-
dagen ganze Rollen von Silbermünzen gefunden haben. Interessant ist ein
rhombischer Messingbeschlag mit Verzierung, der in das 10./11. Jahrhundert
datiert **(Abb. 20)**.

Ein besonderer Fund ist ein Siegelring aus Messing, der in einem wap-
penförmigen Feld die Initialen M v H führt **(Abb. 21)**. Dieser Ring könnte
Mathes von Hönningen (gest. 1576) gehört haben, der als Burgmanne auf
der Henneburg saß. Ebenso bemerkenswert ist ein vergoldeter Bronzeanhänger mit einem runden Wappenfeld, auf dem eine Henne abgebildet ist
(Abb. 22). Das Besondere daran ist seine Verbindung mit dem Henneberger
Herrschaftshaus, das im Wappen eine Henne trägt. Der Anhänger stammt
aus einem Kontext des 12./frühen 13. Jahrhunderts, wurde also in der Regierungszeit Poppos VII. und seiner Gemahlin Jutta getragen. Die Vergoldung
spricht dafür, dass er einer Person in gehobener Stellung gehört hat.

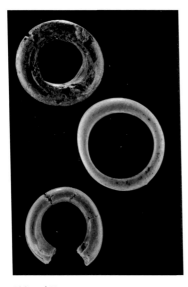

Weiterhin wurden auch Teile von Bronzegefäßen geborgen, außerdem eine Bronzeglocke und eine bronzene Spitze. Unter den Funden sind Glasscherben von Hohlglasgefäßen und Flachglasscheiben und auch Glasringe kommen in einer auffallend hohen Stückzahl vor (Abb. 23). Sonst sind sie auf Thüringer Burgen relativ selten und weisen auf eine eigene Werkstatt im Umfeld von Henneberg hin.

Unter den Lesefunden aus dem Südteil der Grabungsfläche befindet sich ein Werkstein aus gelb-rötlichem Buntsandstein mit einem Schachbrettmuster (Abb. 24). Solche Steine waren seit dem frühen 12. Jahrhundert weit verbreitet und

Abb. 23 | Fig. 23:
Die 16 gefundenen Glasringe datieren in das 12./13. Jahrhundert
16 glass rings dating back to the 12–13th century

Abb. 24 | Fig. 24:
Der Schachbrettstein aus dem 12. Jahrhundert zierte einst die Kapelle auf der Burg
The 12th century ashlar with a chessboard pattern decorated once the castle chapel

wurden nur in Sakralbauten verwendet. Sie kommen auffallend zahlreich in romanischen Klosterkirchen der Benediktiner und Prämonstratenser vor, so auch im Hauskloster der Henneberger Grafen in Veßra, Lkr. Hildburghausen, das 1131 von Gotebold von Henneberg (gest. 1144) gegründet wurde.

Im äußerst umfangreichen Tierknochenbestand sind auch aus Knochen und Geweih gefertigte Gegenstände wie Würfel, Kämme, Zierplättchen, Spielsteine, eine Perle

Abb. 25 | Fig. 25:
Zu den Funden aus Knochen gehört auch ein Würfel
Amongst the bone finds there is also a dice

und ein Knopf vertreten (**Abb. 25**). Das gesamte Knochenmaterial wurde archäozoologisch bearbeitet. Es eignet sich gut, die Essgewohnheiten der auf der Burg lebenden Menschen nachzuvollziehen. Der überwiegende Teil der Tierknochen stammte von Hausschweinen. Schafe bzw. Ziegen und Rinder wurden deutlich weniger verzehrt, ebenso Geflügel und sehr selten Wildtiere und Fische. Auch Pferde, Esel, Katzen und Hunde lebten auf der Burg.

Im Fundmaterial überwiegen die Tiere mit qualitativ hochwertigem Fleisch. Im Vergleich zu anderen mittelalterlichen Burgen Thüringens nimmt die Burg Henneberg im hohen und späten Mittelalter einen Spitzenplatz beim Verzehr hochwertiger Nahrung ein und rangiert noch vor der Wartburg bei Eisenach. Dieses Ergebnis impliziert für das Mittelalter eine überwiegend sozial bessergestellte und demnach wohl auch ökonomisch abgesicherte Personengruppe innerhalb der Burg Henneberg.

Rundgang

Der mächtige Torso des Bergfrieds und die weitgehend geschlossene Ringmaueranlage stellen heute die am besten erhaltenen Bauteile dar. Daneben stehen ein kleiner Wohnbau im Norden sowie ein südlich davon gelegener Rest der Hofmauer eines unterkellerten Gebäudes. Der übrige, ehemals sehr umfängliche Baubestand ist teils durch Grabungen erschlossen und als Grundmauern sichtbar, teils durch ältere Aufnahmen überliefert sowie durch vielfältige Spuren an der **Ringmauer** erkennbar (**Abb. 26**). Diese hat eine Gesamtlänge von etwa 300 Metern und ist teilweise bis in eine Höhe von zehn Metern über dem Felssockel erhalten. Variierende Mauerstärken von 0,75 bis 1,25 Metern verweisen – wie auch diverse Gefügewechsel, Baunähte und zweitverwendete (Werk-)Steine – auf eine mehrphasige Entstehung. Von einem längeren Teilstück im Nordwesten abgesehen, das noch aus dem 13. Jahrhundert stammt, scheint die Ringmauer im späten Mittelalter weitgehend erneuert worden zu sein. Umfangreichere Instandsetzungen erfolgten zwischen 1999 und 2002.

An den höher erhaltenen Mauerzügen finden sich umfängliche Spuren innenseitig ehemals angelehnter Bauten. Dazu gehören Balken- und Rüstlöcher, Fenster- und Schlitzöffnungen, Aborterker und Kamine. Diese zeigen die hohe Dichte von Burgmannensitzen, von denen immerhin 15 für das 14. Jahrhundert erwähnt werden. Die Ringmauer war wohl nahezu über die gesamte Länge auf der Innenseite bebaut, wie der von Ernst Abesser 1880 bis 1883 erstellte Plan mit zahlreichen spätmittelalterlichen Gebäuden an ihrem Rand zeigt (siehe Abb. 3). Insgesamt ist eine genaue zeitliche Einordnung der verschiedenen Ringmauerabschnitte in den seltensten Fällen möglich, da datierbare Elemente fast völlig fehlen und das Mauerwerkgefüge vielfach bei den seit 1990 stattgefundenen Instandsetzungen überformt wurde.

Man betritt das Burggelände heute durch ein im Nordosten liegendes **Tor** (**17; Abb. 27**). Es wurde um 1500 als viertes Tor nachträglich zwischen zwei ältere Ringmauerabschnitte eingefügt. Das erste Tor bestand im Hochmittelalter im Süden der Burganlage (**20**), das zweite (das Zangentor; **3**) nordöstlich des Palas. Im 13. Jahrhundert wurde es abgelöst von Tor Nr. 3 (**16**) etwa

Abb. 26 | Fig. 26:
Der Nordteil der Burg mit einigen ergrabenen Mauerfundamenten
The northern part of the castle with several excavated fundaments

zehn Meter nördlich des heutigen Zugangs. Dieser liegt leicht nach innen versetzt. Auf der Hofseite sind noch die beiden oberen Drehzapfensteine der Torflügel erhalten. Die beiden nach innen verlaufenden Wangenmauern deuten auf einen kleinen Torturm hin. Sie weisen deutliche Brandspuren auf, die vermutlich mit der Erstürmung der Burg im Bauernkrieg 1525 zusammenhängen. Der vor dem Tor befindliche Burggraben – heute ist an dieser Stelle eine Rampe aufgeschüttet – wurde ehemals mit einer Brücke überquert, von der noch um 1700 ein Pfeiler erhalten war.

Genau gegenüber liegen die imposanten Reste des Bergfrieds (**Bergfried II; 18**) mit einem Durchmesser von 14 Metern. Sein Untergeschoss ist durch einen im 18. Jahrhundert erfolgten Durchbruch an der Nordostseite zugänglich. Es wird von einer zehn Meter hohen Kuppel überwölbt, die aus plattigen Bruchsteinen besteht. In ihrem Scheitel befindet sich eine kreisrunde Öffnung, die ursprünglich den einzigen Zugang in das Untergeschoss darstellte (**Abb. 28**).

Abb. 27 | Fig. 27:
Der heutige Zugang. Hinter der Bank befand sich vermutlich das dritte Burgtor
The present castle gate. Behind the bench probably the third castle gate was located

Abb. 28 | Fig. 28:
Blick in das Erdgeschoss des Bergfrieds mit dem ursprünglich einzigen Zugang
im Scheitel des Kuppelgewölbes
View of the ground floor of the keep with the original only access in the apex
of the domed vault

Abb. 29 | Fig. 29:
Die Kemenate an der Nordseite der Ringmauer
The Kemenate in the northern part of the curtain wall

Die Datierung des Bergfrieds in die Mitte bis zweite Hälfte des 13. Jahrhunderts ergibt sich aus der verhältnismäßig nachlässigen Qualität des Mauerwerks, das man nicht aus Werkstein- oder Buckelquadern fügte, wie es andere Türme von Henneberger Burgen zeigen, sondern aus Hausteinquadern. Auffallend unregelmäßig ist zudem das Mauerwerkgefüge mit den „wellig" wirkenden Lagerfugen und einzelnen Versprüngen. Im Jahr 1885 wurde der Bergfried als Aussichtsturm hergerichtet und mit einer Treppe erschlossen. Eine Erneuerung der Treppenanlage und der Plattform erfolgte 1999.

Etwa in der Mitte der nördlichen Ringmauer erhebt sich ein zweigeschossiger rechteckiger Wohnbau – eine **Kemenate (8)** –, der als Sitz eines der zahlreichen Burgmannen anzusehen ist. Im Erdgeschoss befindet sich nördlich ein kleines romanisches Mono- oder Biforium (**Abb. 29**). Das Fenster wurde wahrscheinlich im 19. Jahrhundert hier eingefügt. Darauf lassen die Zweiteilung des Gewändes und Zerstörungsspuren an diesem sowie das zweifellos

Abb. 30 | Fig. 30:
Die Kemenate der Familie von Trott
The Kemenate of the von Trott family

Abb. 31 | Fig. 31:
Der Rundbogen der Holzstube mit den kleinen Fensteröffnungen
The arch of the Holzstube with small window openings

spätmittelalterliche Mauerwerk des Wohnbaus schließen (14./15. Jahrhundert).

Östlich dieser Kemenate befindet sich der **Burgbrunnen (4)**. Er hat einen Durchmesser von 2,50 Metern und wurde in den anstehenden Muschelkalk gearbeitet. Im oberen Teil ist er mit grob bearbeiteten Steinen ausgekleidet. Der Brunnen wurde 1996 untersucht und bis in eine Tiefe von 12,80 Metern entleert. Seine Gesamttiefe konnte jedoch nicht ermittelt werden. Im 15. Jahrhundert war er mit einem Brunnenhaus überbaut worden, das sich archäologisch nachweisen ließ. Südlich des Brunnens liegen die Reste einer weiteren **Kemenate (9)**, von der der Zugang in den Keller erhalten geblieben ist. Sie stammt aus dem späten 14./15. Jahrhundert und war der Wohnsitz der Burgmannenfamilie von Trott. An ihrer Südwestwand ist noch der Anschlag des Riegels der umgebauten Hoftoranlage zu sehen **(Abb. 30)**.

Von dem herrschaftlichen Wohnsitz im Nordwesten der Burganlage sind noch einige bedeutsame Reste erhalten oder ergrabene Mauerzüge

auf der Geländeoberfläche rekonstruiert. Auffällig ist vor allem ein großer, etwa acht Meter spannender Rundbogen aus Muschelkalk-Werksteinquadern in der Ringmauer, der sowohl an der Außen- als auch der Innenseite sichtbar ist (**Abb. 31**). In seinem Binnenfeld befinden sich in drei Reihen zum Teil zugemauerte Fensteröffnungen – oben zwei, in der Mitte drei, unten vier –, die in etwa ein Dreieck bilden. Sie sind die Reste einer **Holzstube (14)**, die eine Rarität im Burgenbau darstellt. Die Funktion solcher Holzstuben bestand in der Speicherung von Wärme. Um sie nicht nach außen dringen zu lassen, waren die Fenster klein, dafür aber in einer höheren Stückzahl vorhanden. Beheizt wurde die Henneberger Holzstube vermutlich mit beweglichen Wärmequellen wie zum Beispiel Wärmeschalen. Hinweise auf eine Fußbodenheizung oder einen Kachelofen fanden sich nicht. 1992 wurde an einem der Fenster ein hölzerner Fensterrahmen entdeckt. Er war aus Tannenholz gearbeitet und datiert anhand dendrochronologischer Untersuchungen in das Jahr 1295 (**Abb. 32**). Drei weitere Holzbalken ergaben Dendrodaten im Zeitraum zwischen 1295 und

Abb. 32 | Fig. 32:
Das Holzfenster von 1295 ist eines der ältesten Holzfenster in Deutschland
The wooden window from 1295 is one of the oldest wooden windows in Germany

Abb. 33 | Fig. 33:
Roland Weibezahl, der spätgotische Wohnbau von Südosten, Federzeichnung, 1858
Roland Weibezahl, the late medieval residential building in the south-east, pen and ink drawing, 1858

1305. Damit ist die Henneberger Holzstube eine der ältesten auf Burgen im deutschsprachigen Raum.

Brandspuren auf der Innenseite des Mauerwerks belegen ein Feuer, das das Erd- und Obergeschoss erfasste. Im späten Mittelalter wurde die Holzstube entfernt. Man setzte die Fenster der oberen und unteren Reihe zu und fügte fünf vorn abgerundete Kragsteine ein, von denen die beiden mittleren in den Fensteröffnungen der oberen Reihe sitzen; der südlichste Kragstein wird vom Ansatz einer Quermauer überschnitten und bezeugt damit deren nachträgliche Entstehung. Das kleine Rechteckfenster nördlich des Bogens ist im 19. Jahrhundert anstelle eines Ausbruchs eingesetzt worden.

Ein weiterer interessanter Befund zeigt sich im nur fragmentarisch erhaltenen Obergeschoss über der Holzstube. Dieses war mit einem ungewöhnlich repräsentativen vierbahnigen Gruppenfenster zur Landschaft hin

42   **Abb. 34 | Fig. 34:**
Der Palas wurde im 15. Jahrhundert umgebaut
The residential building was rebuilt in the 15th century

Abb. 35 | Fig. 35:
Der Ringmauerabschnitt südlich der Holzstube
The section of the curtain wall south of the Holzstube

geöffnet, dessen Einzelformen durch zahlreiche Abbildungen bekannt sind (zuerst bei Christian Juncker 1703, siehe Abb. 14). Es sind vier aus gelbem Buntsandstein gefertigte gleiche, durch Mittelstäbe geteilte Fensterbahnen mit kleeblattförmigem Schluss, die auch im 19. Jahrhundert auf zahlreichen Grafiken dargestellt wurden **(Abb. 33)**. Man darf dieses Fenster aufgrund seiner aufwendigen Form einem reich ausgestatteten herrschaftlichen Wohnraum oder einem Saal zuweisen. Von diesem Gruppenfenster hat sich nur das Gewändefragment der südlichen Fensterbahn erhalten.

Östlich der Holzstube sind noch die Grundmauern des im 14. Jahrhundert an den **Kapellenturm (15)** aus dem 13. Jahrhundert angebauten Chorabschlusses und des anschließenden trapezförmigen Gebäudes **(12; Gebäude IX)** erkennbar. Nördlich befindet sich ein **Rundturm (13)** aus dem frühen 13. Jahrhundert. Er wurde im 19. Jahrhundert auf seinen alten Fundamentmauern rekonstruiert. Als im 15. Jahrhundert der ältere Wohnbau **(1; Palas)** nach Süden und Osten erweitert wurde, brach man den Rundturm teilweise ab

Abb. 36 | Fig. 36:
Der südliche Ringmauerbereich
The southern curtain wall area

und überwölbte die entstandene Halbschale. Das neue Gebäude erhielt ein Obergeschoss, dessen Südwand sich auch heute noch in Höhe der Plattform deutlich abzeichnet **(Abb. 34)**. Nach Westen öffnete es sich mit zwei zwei-bahnigen Rechteckfenstern; von einem dritten Fenster ist nur ein Gewän-defragment am Nordende der Mauer erhalten geblieben. Das Obergeschoss hatte ebenso wie das Untergeschoss aus dem 13./14. Jahrhundert einen Kamin, für den der alte Schlot aufgestockt wurde. Er ist auf der Außenseite noch gut erkennbar (siehe Abb. 9). Der spätgotische Wohnbau brannte im Bauernkrieg 1525 aus, worauf Brandspuren im Erd- und Obergeschoss der Westwand hinweisen.

Etwa in der **Mitte der Westseite** springt die Ringmauer rechtwinklig um 4,50 Meter aus, um nach einem zweiten rechtwinkligen Knick weiter nach Norden zu verlaufen. An dieser Stelle befand sich im 14. Jahrhundert ein Ge-bäude, dessen Ost-, Süd- und Westmauern noch erhalten sind (heute be-findet sich hier ein Einbau von 1996). Das anschließende, zweigeschossig er-

Abb. 37 | Fig. 37:
Im Süden der Ringmauer wurde der hochmittelalterliche Rundturm nachgebildet
In the southern part of the curtain wall the round tower was reconstructed

haltene Mauerstück stammt aus der Zeit um 1300 und weist im Erdgeschoss einen als Öffnung erscheinenden Aborterker auf, der von einem Schlitzfenster und einem kleinen Rechteckfenster flankiert wird (**Abb. 35**). Im Obergeschoss deutet ein zweibahniges Spitzbogenfenster auf einen Wohnbereich hin. Das Gewände zeigt außen Löcher für Fensterläden. Unmittelbar südlich des Fensters ist eine Nische aus der Mauer ausgespart, die als Wandschrank anzusehen ist. Die Innenseite der Mauer weist Brandspuren auf.

Am **südlichen Ringmauerabschnitt** sind ebenfalls Reste der Innenbebauung erhalten geblieben (**Abb. 36**). Ein horizontaler Absatz markiert die Lage der Decke zwischen dem verschütteten Keller- und dem Erdgeschoss. Dazu gehören auch einige Vertiefungen, in denen die Holzbalken der Decke lagen. Der Keller wurde durch zwei Schlitzfenster belüftet, die auf der Außenseite sichtbar sind. Zum Erdgeschoss gehörte ein größeres Fenster. Östlich davon sind noch Abrisspuren einer Quermauer zu sehen, die den Raum oder das

Abb. 38 | Fig. 38:
In der östlichen Ringmauer sind zahlreiche Spolien verbaut
Numerous spolia are built into the eastern curtain wall

Gebäude nach Osten begrenzte. Westlich des Fensters befindet sich ein Schlitzfenster, begleitet von einer Lichtnische. Es folgen ein zugesetzter Aborterker, dessen nördliche Laibung mit einer zweiten Quermauer abschließt, sowie zwei weitere Schlitzfenster. Vom Obergeschoss zeugen der untere Teil eines Fensters sowie ein Kamin, von dem zwei Kragsteine des Rauchfangs erhalten geblieben sind. Vermutlich steht der eben beschriebene Mauerabschnitt mit den beiden überlieferten Ringmauererneuerungen 1489 und 1516 in Verbindung.

Im Südosten zeigt der Mauerverlauf eine Ausbuchtung. Hier hat man 2001/02 bei der Instandsetzung der Mauer den um 1000 erbauten hochmittelalterlichen Rundturm **(19; Bergfried I)** als Halbrund nachgebildet, was vor allem auf der Außenseite gut erkennbar ist **(Abb. 37)**. Im Jahr 1845 wurden im südlichen Außenbereich der Westmauer Teile mit einer Mauervorlage aus zwei Stützpfeilern und dazwischen eingezogenem Bogen unterfangen.

Abb. 39 | Fig. 39:
Zugemauerte Aborterker an der Außenseite der südöstlichen Ringmauer
Walled-up garderobes on the outside of the south-eastern curtain wall

Von der ursprünglichen Innenbebauung im **Osten der Burganlage** zeugen heute nur noch einige Balkenlöcher, Fensteröffnungen und Aborterker. Zahlreihe Werksteine sind sekundär in der Mauer verbaut worden, unter anderem drei nur auf der Außenseite in großer Höhe sichtbare, zu einem Rundbogenfenster gehörende Stücke, die eine mit Halbkugeln besetzte Fase aufweisen und ursprünglich zu einem spätromanischen Wohnbau gehörten **(Abb. 38)**. Die nächsten Vergleiche für Rundbogenfenster mit einem derartigen Kugelbesatz findet man in der Marktapotheke in Saalfeld, Lkr. Saalfeld-Rudolstadt. Etwas weiter südlich lassen sich noch drei Aborterker ausmachen, zwei davon zugesetzt. An der Außenseite sind die abgeschlagenen zugehörigen Kragsteinpaare noch deutlich erkennbar **(Abb. 39)**. Das Mauerstück datiert vermutlich ins 14./15. Jahrhundert.

Durch ihre Lage an der innerdeutschen Grenze war die Burg Henneberg in den letzten Jahrzehnten des 20. Jahrhunderts etwas in Vergessenheit geraten, was sich mit der Wiedervereinigung änderte. Archäologische Grabungen sowie die Arbeit von Historikern und Bauforschern in den 1990er Jahren bis 2002 haben unser Wissen über diese bedeutende Burganlage enorm erweitert. Die spätmittelalterliche Ringmauer, der mächtige Bergfried oder die Holzstube, die zu den ältesten Bauten dieser Art im deutschsprachigen Raum zählt, künden noch heute von der Bedeutung der Henneberger Grafen, die im Hoch- und Spätmittelalter nicht nur die Geschichte Südthüringens und Unterfrankens entscheidend prägten, sondern unter Berthold VII. auch eine herausragende Rolle in der Reichsgeschichte spielten.

Aufgaben und Ziele

Die Burgruine Henneberg zählt zu den bedeutenden Zeugnissen einer längst vergangenen Dynastie, den Henneberger Grafen. Wie bei aufgegebenen Anlagen häufig, haben sich nur noch Teile der ehemaligen Burg erhalten. Von den ursprünglichen Gebäuden sind lediglich noch einige Grundmauern vorhanden. Sichtbarstes Zeichen sind Reste des Bergfrieds, den die Stiftung Thüringer Schlösser vor gut 20 Jahren wieder begehbar gemacht hat, sowie Umfassungsmauern, eine Wand der Kemenate, Reste der Kapelle und des kleinen Rundturms. Die während der Sanierung begleitend durchgeführten archäologischen Grabungen des Thüringischen Landesamts für Denkmalpflege haben wesentlich zur Erhellung des historischen Bestands beigetragen.

Die Burg ist öffentlich zugänglich und wird vor allem von Wanderern aufgesucht, meist als Etappe auf dem Weg durch das Grabfeld und entlang des überregionalen Wegs „Grünes Band". Um die für Südthüringen und das nördliche Unterfranken historisch bedeutsame Anlage aufzuwerten, sollen künftig die Ergebnisse der archäologischen Untersuchungen anschaulich vermittelt werden und damit Besucherinnen und Besuchern die einstige Bedeutung der Stammburg der gefürsteten Henneberger Grafen näherbringen. Dieses Projekt ist in Zusammenarbeit mit dem Thüringischen Landesamt für Denkmalpflege und Archäologie geplant.

Die Stiftung erhält die 1995 in ihren Bestand übertragene Ruinenanlage im Rahmen ihres Ruinenpflegewerks. Der Mauerbestand wird bezüglich seines Erhaltungszustands regelmäßig überprüft und im Bedarfsfall werden Sicherungsmaßnahmen durchgeführt. Zur Gewährleistung der Sichtachsen auf die Burg wird auch umfänglich Bewuchs außerhalb des Burggeländes entfernt.

Ehrenamtlich wird die Burgruine durch den 1990 gegründeten Club Henneberg e. V. betreut. Der Verein kümmert sich um die laufende Pflege der Anlage und bietet Veranstaltungen an, darunter das alle zwei Jahre stattfindende Burgfest, ist aber auch vor Ort Ansprechpartner als ehrenamtliche Schlossverwaltung für Belange im Auftrag der Stiftung Thüringer Schlösser und Gärten.

Zeittafel

7./6. Jh. v. Chr.	Bau einer ersten Befestigungsanlage auf dem Schlossberg
2. H. 10. Jh.	Gründung der Burg unter den Schweinfurter Grafen am nördlichen Randbereich ihrer Herrschaft; aus dieser Zeit stammen die Gebäude I–III, IV (Wohnturm), V und VI und vermutlich der Brunnen
um 1000/30	Errichtung des ersten Rundturms im Süden der Burg; es existiert eine erste Ringmauer, das Tor befindet sich vermutlich im Süden der Burganlage
1096	Erste urkundliche Erwähnung eines Henneberger Grafen (Gotebold II.)
1190	Teilung der Herrschaft in die Linie Henneberg sowie die Seitenlinien Botenlauben und Strauf
um 1200	Der erste Rundturm wird abgetragen und der Zugang zur Burg nach Nordwesten verlegt (Zangentor = zweites Tor)
1221	Erste direkte urkundliche Erwähnung der Burg Henneberg als „castrum"
1. H. 13. Jh.	Größere Umbaumaßnahmen unter Poppo VII. und seiner Frau Jutta: Palas I, kleiner Rundturm und Hoftoranlage im Nordwesten der Burg, Einbau einer Kapelle in den Wohnturm
nach 1245	Poppos Sohn Berthold aus erster Ehe erbt die Stammburg und den größten Teil des väterlichen Besitzes; unter Sohn Hermann aus zweiter Ehe entsteht die „Neue Herrschaft Henneberg"
1253	Ersterwähnung eines Kaplans
um 1250	Bau des großen Bergfrieds

1274	Teilung der Herrschaft in die Linien Schleusingen, Aschach und Hartenberg-Römhild; die Henneburg fällt an Berthold V.
13. Jh.	Abtragung der ersten Ringmauer, Verkleinerung des Burgplateaus, Errichtung einer neuen Ringmauer unter Einbeziehung des Palas, des Rundturms und der Holzstube; Errichtung eines Zwingers im Norden und Verlegung des Burgtors (drittes Tor) in die Nähe des heutigen Zugangs
um 1300	Bau der Holzstube
Ende 13./ Anf. 14. Jh.	Unter Berthold VII. Verlagerung des Herrschaftsschwerpunkts nach Schleusingen, Umbau der Burg Henneberg zur militärischen Feste
1308	Beschädigung eines Turms durch Blitzschlag (Kapellenturm, evtl. auch kleiner Rundturm), danach Errichtung des trapezförmigen Gebäudes (Gebäude IX) und Umbau der Südwand des Palas unter Einbeziehung des Rundturms
um 1330	15 urkundlich erwähnte Burgmannen bezeugen die Gefährdung der Burg in dieser Zeit
1393	Graf Heinrich X. von Henneberg-Schleusingen versetzt seinem Schwiegersohn Friedrich I. aus der Linie Römhild eine Hälfte der Burg bis zur Zahlung einer Mitgift
1432	Aufteilung der Burg unter den Söhnen Heinrichs X. und Friedrichs I.
15. Jh.	Der Palas wird durch einen Brand beschädigt, danach Umbau und Erweiterung nach Süden und Osten (Arkaden), das Obergeschoss hat drei zweibahnige Rechteckfenster und einen Kamin; Bau des Brunnenhauses und der Kemenate der Familie von Trott, Umbau der Hoftoranlage
1489 und 1516	Umfassende Erneuerung der Ringmauer, Verlegung des Burgtors an die heutige Stelle (viertes Tor)
1525	Zerstörung der Burg durch aufständische Bauern

Mitte 16. Jh.	Erste Abbrucharbeiten an der Burg und besonders am Bergfried; Weiterverwendung des Materials
Ende 16. Jh.	Burkhard Hermann von Trott ist der einzige noch auf der Burg ansässige Burgmann
18. Jh.	Das Untergeschoss des Bergfrieds erhält einen Eingang
1784	Planierung des Burghofs durch Herzog Georg I.
ab 1843	Landbaumeister August Wilhelm Döbner führt erste Sicherungsmaßnahmen durch
1879–1883	Sanierungs- und Freilegungsarbeiten durch Ernst Abesser; er erstellt einen ersten Gesamtplan der Burg
um 1935	Ausgrabungen durch Friedrich Tenner
1992–1995	Archäologische Ausgrabungen im Nordwesten der Burg und teilweise Rekonstruktion der freigelegten Fundamentmauern
2001/02	Sanierung der südöstlichen Ringmauer mit begleitenden archäologischen Untersuchungen; der dabei entdeckte hochmittelalterliche Rundturm wird im Mauerverlauf kenntlich gemacht

Location and history of research

Henneberg is located about 10 km south-west of Meiningen, on the road from Würzburg to Meiningen, directly on the border to Bavaria and in the watershed of the Upper Main and the Werra. (fig. 1) This road, often referred to as 'Hohe Straße' (High Road), is an old trading route between Central Germany and south German region of Franconia. Henneberg castle occupies the whole peak of a muschelkalk hill, the so called 'Schlossberg' (Castle Hill), east of the town of Henneberg. (fig. 2) With the height of 527 m ASL, it towers about 130 m over the surrounding area, rivalled only by the 530 m high 'Heilige Berg' (Holy Hill), located 800 m to the north-east, and the 505 m high 'Wolfsberg' (Wolf Hill) in the south-west.

Historically the region around Henneberg belongs to the settlement area of 'Grabfeldgau', which is composed out of parts of the following districts: Lower Franconian district of Rhön-Grabfeld and districts of Schmalkalden-Meiningen and Hildburghausen. It covers a region between the Franconian Saale in the south and the middle reaches of the Werra in the north. It is flanked by the Kuppen hills of the Rhön mountains in the west and the two Gleichbergen in the east. Henneberg is located in the northern part of the 'Grabfeldgau' area.

The fortification is situated on a mountain spur oriented north-south, which levels out direction south. The whole plateau is surrounded by a curtain wall. The area encompassed within measures 120 m (north-south) to 65 m (west-east), narrowing down to 20 m in the most southern part. The castle grounds are protected by a system of ditch-rampart defences, strengthened by two additional ditches and ramparts in the south.

Since 1845 various excavation and conservation works have taken place. At the end of the 19th century numerous foundations along the curtain wall were unearthed by a local master builder, Ernst Abesser, and a site plan was drawn. (fig. 3) Abesser had only removed the upper soil layers when he encountered the first remains of foundations, uncovering mainly the late medieval parts. Fortunately for the generations of researchers that followed, he did not disturb the prehistoric and high medieval layers of the 10th–13th century.

Further examinations were carried out in 1936 by Friedrich Tenner, the leader of the Henneberg-Franconian Historical Society. The reunification of Germany and opening of the previously restricted inner German border area, within which the castle was located, was followed by four excavation campaigns conducted between 1992 and 1995 in the north-west part of the castle by Thuringian State Office for the Preservation of Historical Monuments and Archaeology in cooperation with the Otto Friedrich University of Bamberg and the Martin Luther University of Halle-Wittenberg. During that time an area of about 750 m² was examined and some preliminary reports were published. In 2001 the Palace, Castle and Gardens Trust of Thuringia initiated a restoration of the south-east curtain wall, also accompanied by archaeological examinations. According to the recent state of research five building phases can be accounted for – one in the 7–6th century BC, two in the Early till the High Middle Ages and two in the Late Middle Ages. (see plan)

History of the Counts of Henneberg and Henneberg Castle

The Henneberg family were first mentioned in 1096, when Gotebold II, Count of Henneberg, witnessed a barter exchange between the Prince-Bishopric of Würzburg and the Benedictine cloister of Comburg, in the vicinity of Schwäbisch-Hall. At that point the castle had been in existence for almost 100 years, probably having been founded in the 10th century by the counts of Schweinfurt at the northern edge of their territory. The Schweinfurters, whose dominion bordered the Grabfeldgau to the south, supported the building of castles in the northern part of Mainfranken. Apart from Schweinfurt, where the family line had originated, they also owned lands in Grabfeldgau. It seems only logical that they would want to reinforce their dominance over the bordering territories with the help of the local nobility. The future counts of Henneberg were most likely amongst these nobles. The castle was erected on the Schlossberg of Hennerberg in the 2nd half of the 10th century, exactly at the same time when Count Berthold of Schweinfurt and his son Heinrich needed to strengthen their power against the Church of Würzburg and the monarchy.

The territory they owned consisted of the properties of the Babenberger (Bamberg Castle in Franconia), who were the ancestors of Poppo I, the first known count of Henneberg. Their imperial fief was located in Thuringian Forest between the rivers Schleuse and Hasel and further at Lichtenberg Castle and its surroundings. In addition, since the late 11th century the Hennebergs held the office of the burgrave of Würzburg and the Prince-Bishopric of Würzburg and could, therefore, influence the imperial politics. It was Gotebold II (died in 1144) who laid the foundations for the future importance of his House. He moved the centre of his domain direction east, followed by founding of the monastery in Veßra in 1131. Gotebold II strove for a consolidated territory between Schleusingen and Henneberg. As a result the ancestral castle found itself on the margin of the dominion. By inheriting the territory of Nordeck (Zella-Mehlis, Thuringia) in the 2nd half of the 12th century the counts of Henneberg acquired influence to the north-east. The lands stayed continuously in their possession until the middle of the 13th century. However, already in 1190 the house divided into the line of Henneberg and the collateral lines of Botenlauben and Strauf.

The first direct documented reference to the castle as '*castrum*' appeared in 1221. Between 1220 and 1274, under Poppo VII (died in 1245) and his wife Jutta, the widow of Dietrich der Bedrängte ('the Opressed'), Margrave of Meissen (died in 1221), a brief period of prosperity followed. It was accompanied by a brisk building activity at the castle, which can be supported by archaeological research. The castle as the main seat seems to have satisfied the requirements of Jutta, who descended from the Landgraves of Thuringia. It fits this picture that on a 1253 document Albert, chaplain of Henneberg, is mentioned among the witnesses. Also the existence of a castle chapel, proven through archaeological research, seems to further substantiate this claim. According to a 1464 document it was dedicated to Saint Catherine.

In 1246 the collateral line of Coburg separated under Hermann I. In 1274 followed the further division of the countship into the lines of Schleusingen, Aschach and Hartenberg-Römhild. Henneburg passed into the hands of Berthold V (died in 1284), the founder of the Henneberg-Schleusingen line. His son Berthold VII (died in 1340) was the most outstanding representative of the new line. He played an important part in the imperial politics and was an advisor to kings and emperors. It was Berthold VII who moved the family seat to Schleusingen which resulted in Henneberg losing its importance as a representative residence. Simultaneously, its significance as a military stronghold was increasing on account of the ability to control the road from Mellrichstadt to Meiningen, both in possession of the bishop of Würzburg. Due to this change in function extensive building activities took place in the castle.

In 1393 a part of the castle was given as a dowry to the Henneberg-Römhild line and remained with them until the line's extinction. In May 1393 count Heinrich X of Henneberg-Schleusingen married his daughter off to count Friedrich I of the Römhild line. Since he could or would not pay the dowry of 4000 guilders, he transferred the deeds to a half of Henneberg onto his son-in-law and the property was to remain in his possession until the sum was paid off. Friedrich and his heirs could use the castle according to their will and, what follows, for any political or military purpose. Since the above-mentioned dowry was not paid, the castle was divided between the sons of Heinrich and Friedrich in April 1432. This probably significantly reduced the importance of the castle as a residence and military stronghold, as important decisions from then on had to be coordinated with the relatives, who did not always have the same territorial-political interests.

In 1525 the castle was destroyed as a direct result of the Peasants' War. The capture of the castle by the peasant army, who had no artillery, shows that in the age of firearms its military value was marginal. Rebuilding was briefly considered in 1527, but was not carried out. However, until the beginning of the 17th century the castle remained partially inhabited. After the extinction of the Aschach line, the territory went to the Schleusingen line in 1549. With the death of Georg Ernst, Count of Henneberg-Schleusingen, in 1583, the Schleusingen patriline also became extinct. The county together with the castle ruins passed to the Wettin dynasty but they only administered it.

Building history and archaeological excavations

Henneberg Castle – a hilltop settlement of the 7–6th century BC

The castle hill was first used as a dwelling in the 7–6th century BC. Two ditches, numerous post holes carved in the rock and a settlement layer are what remains of a hilltop settlement of the Hallstatt culture. It is not possible to attempt a reconstruction of the layout of houses basing on the documented post holes. A simple, 0.4 m deep ditch was unearthed in the northwest of the excavation area. It was carved in the limestone and served as foundation for a palisade or a massive fence. It had the length of about 13 m and curved over the plateau and, therefore, did not follow the slope side directly. (fig. 4) It was interrupted by two massive post holes for enabling access, maybe through a gate, which was not wider than 0.8 m. Such a narrow entrance could not have been the primary one.

Another, unfortunately disrupted, ditch was located in the south of the excavation area and stretched from south-east to north-west, therefore, roughly across the plateau. With the bottom width of about 1.5 m and the depth of up to 0.7 m it was considerably larger than the palisade ditch described above. It was filled with numerous limestone slabs. The ditch was most likely a part of a defence system. The same can probably be said about the triple rampart-ditch system located in front of the medieval neck ditch. However, its exact dating cannot be established.

The High Medieval building phases

From the middle of the 10th century Schlossberg of Henneberg was systematically developed into a castle complex. All this took place c. 100 years before the name of the Henneberg family appeared in written sources. No knowledge about these high medieval fortifications existed before the excavation campaigns of 1992–1995 and 2001–2002. The examinations conducted by Ernst Abesser in the 19th century and Friedrich Tenner in 1936 did not reveal anything about the presence of a high medieval settlement.

Two high medieval building phases were recorded within the north-western and southern excavation area. The former is located on the highest point of the plateau. A 7.5 to 7.5 m large half-timbered building, erected on the highest point of the inner area in the 2nd half of the 10th century, belongs to the first building phase. **(1; Building I)** The wooden structure burned down.

On its west side it was connected to another **building (6; Building II)**, of whose foundations only the lowest layer of mortar remained, covering an area of about 9 × 3 m. Between these two buildings two fireplaces, used in the early 11th century, were located.

The second building phase lasted from the middle of the 11th to the beginning of the 13th century. Under Gotebold II (died in 1144) not only were the foundations for the House of Henneberg with its extensive properties laid, but also a very animated building activity on the castle developed.

In his place of residence, after demolishing Building I, in the north-west of the castle a 9.0 to 9.0 m large half-timbered building with an annex to the south was erected on the highest point. **(1; Building III)** This building was subsequently demolished at the beginning of the 13th century. The stonework was 0.9 m wide and carried out in herringbone pattern (*opus spicatum*). **(fig. 5)** The building had green glass windows and was covered with pointed roof tiles and white glazed ridge tiles. **(fig. 6)** To the south it was connected to a 10 to 10 m large residential building **(15; Building IV)**, which was made of small ashlars and roofed in the same manner as Building III. **(fig. 7)** It would have been a building entirely made of stone, with the wall thickness of about 1.70 metres. No information can be provided about its internal structure. It was a tower house built in the High Middle Ages and was in use since the beginning of the 13th century as a chapel tower, and since the 14th century as a chapel.

Another building **(1; Building V)** was located directly north of Building III. It was predominantly made of red and light yellow sandstone and had an inner plan of 4.3 to 3.5 m. Scientific examination dates its construction to about 1100, therefore during the reign of Gotebold II. Adjacent to it, in the north-west, there was an almost square building (3.8 to 3 m) – a small tower **(2; Building VI)** measuring inside only 2.4 to 2 m, possibly topped with a slightly larger half-timbered upper floor. The **well (4)** located in the north was, in all probability, also created in the High Middle Ages.

In the 11th century the southern part of the castle complex was built up as well. A round tower **(Tower I; 19)** of shell rock masonry, whose foundations were uncovered during the excavations and which is considered to be the oldest medieval round tower in Thuringia, dates from around 1000/1030. Its outer diameter was 11.7 m and wall thickness – 2.7 m. (**fig. 8**) It was linked to a wall, at present only 3.4 m long and 0.7 m wide, which is believed to be the oldest curtain wall. This find allows us to assume that already in High Middle Ages the whole area was enclosed by a curtain wall. The **first castle gate (20)** was, in all probability, located next to the round tower. This theory is mainly supported by the topography of the area allowing for a gentle ascent towards the castle from the south-west in contrast to the steep, northern climb, used first in the Late Middle Ages. The access from the south was additionally protected by a double **rampart-ditch system**, which could have been created as early as the Hallstatt period (7–6th century BC). The round tower was demolished not later than at the turn of the 13th century, leading to the question why such a mighty tower should have existed for only about 150 years. About 1200 a part of the cliff collapsed and took with it the first defensive wall, leaving the tower standing directly on the remaining edge. This is the reason why the tower was vacated and demolished. The exposed foundation of the tower was conserved during the restoration of the curtain wall in 2002. It was left in the ground and covered with geotextile.

It would be interesting to compare the Henneburg tower to other castle towers created under the reign of the counts of Henneberg in the 12th century. During the 12th and early 13th century following the example of the ancestral castle of Henneberg (outer diameter of 11.7 m) the castle towers in Botenlauben (north tower, outer diameter 11.2 m), on the Nordeck (outer diameter of c. 12 m) and in Dillstädt (outer diameter of c. 10 m) were created, all made of double shell masonry, executed in small ashlars or chamfered ashlars. The similarities between the four towers are notable and have no parallels in the German speaking area.

After the demolition of the tower, the entrance to the castle was moved to the north-west, there where on the excavation plan two walls of double shell masonry, 1.5 m thick and 2.7 to 2.2 m long, meet. The obtuse-angled wall segment used to be a part of a **pincer gate (3)** with two inward angled walls, typical for the Carolingian and Ottonian castles. Of this gate only parts of the western wall, forming one side of the long alleyway leading towards the castle, could be excavated. Both walls were located outside the present-day curtain wall, on a plateau which was levelled in the Late Middle Ages. Sadly, the eastern part of the gate was destroyed during the excavations of Abesser in the 19th century. During the electromagnetic survey in the north a curved wall leading towards the north-western edge of the plateau came to light. There it reached the pincer gate. Even today at this point the north wall of the late medieval *Kemenate* protrudes from the line of the curtain wall, so it can be assumed that a tower belonging to the high medieval gate complex stood here originally. **(see fig. 29)** At this place the curved line of the high medieval curtain wall can be traced in the rock. Furthermore, there where the pincer gate was located a distinct indentation in the rock can be distinguished.

The footprint of the Hallstatt and the late medieval castle measuring almost 8000 m² was originally much larger than the 5000 m² of today. The rocky plateau was not levelled out until the Late Middle Ages and was gently descending towards the slope. It can be assumed that the edge of the slope was fortified by either a dry stone wall or a rampart or a combination of both.

The Late Medieval building phases

In the Late Middle Ages two building phases can be accounted for as well. They are dated from the 13th to the middle of the 14th century and from then to the early 16th century.

The prestigious residential building (1; *palas*) was in all probability built in connection with the marriage of Poppo VII and Jutta at the beginning of the 13th century. In consequence, the high medieval Buildings III, V and VI were demolished. The *palas* was 13.5 m long and between 7.7 m and 8.5 m wide. In the north it was connected to a tower-like annex. Inside, the sandstone floor was laid in the lime mortar. Originally the building was detached, as can be proven by a sandstone corner joint which in the Late Middle Ages was integrated into the curtain wall. **(fig. 9)**

It is highly probable that directly after building the *palas* the small **round tower (13)** with the outer diameter of 8.7 m and the wall thickness of c. 1.3 m was erected. Poppo VII (died in 1242) was surely also responsible for the construction of a chapel in the 10 to 10 m large tower house. **(15; Building IV)** This is how in the 13th century the chapel tower was created. **(see fig. 7)** The presence of a chaplain was recorded as early as 1253. A 3/5 chancel with two openings towards north-east and north-west was presumably added to the eastern part of the high medieval tower house in the 14th century.

About 9 to 10 m east of the *palas* a **gate complex (10)** was set in a 5 m gap between two almost square buildings, each measuring ca. 2,9 × 2,5 m. Numerous militaria finds near the gate such as spurs, horseshoes, horseshoe nails and arrowheads give evidence to the military character of the castle. **(fig. 10)**

It is debatable if the northern tower **(18; Tower II)** was erected during the reign of Poppo VII or that of his successor Heinrich III (died in 1262) and his sons. According to the most recent studies of architectural history we can place the creation of the keep at about 1250. Since the middle of the 13th century it occupied the central position in the northern part of the castle complex. With its outer diameter of 14 m, the wall thickness of 3.4 m and the inner diameter of 7.2 m the free-standing keep dominated the castle area. Today only the ground floor has remained. Its 14 m high walls are made of red and white sandstones with muschelkalk blocks above them. **(fig. 11)**

Berthold VII (died in 1340) moved the family seat to Schleusingen which resulted in Henneberg losing its importance as a representative residence. Simultaneously, its significance as a military stronghold was increasing. Many new buildings were erected during this time.

In the northwest, south of the small round tower, a building with a cellar and *Holzstube* **(14)** on the ground floor was erected (Building VI). **(see fig. 7)** The *Holzstube* with inner surface of 8.7 to 8.2 m was almost square. The building shows unique architectural features and can principally be found in late medieval castles in South Germany or Bohemia.

Approximately in line with the two square buildings of the gate complex, another gate tower measuring 6 × 6 m **(5; Building VIII)** was built in the 13th century. This was done after the demolition of the pincer gate, parts of which were reused in the construction of the tower.

In 1308 a lightning stroke was recorded, which set fire to the castle and caused one of the large towers to collapse. Burn marks on the rocks between the round tower near the *palas* and the chapel tower suggest that both towers might have collapsed. The round tower was afterwards partially demolished and the southern wall of the *palas* was remodelled to integrate the foundation of the tower. To stabilise the chapel tower, an equilateral triangular wall was added in the northwest. By extending one side to the north-east and adding a wall running from north-west to south-east, which bordered the foundation of the former gateway, a trapezoidal building **(12; Building IX)** was created with an entrance to the courtyard in the north-west. **(see fig. 7)** The excavation results suggest it was a timber-framed construction.

In the early 13th century the southern part of the castle was used as a building area **(21)**. Stones, most likely for the construction of the palas, were cut and worked there. Later, at the end of the 13th century, a square building **(22; Building X)** was erected on the site, of which only a 6 to 5 m section has survived until today. After the archaeological investigation it was backfilled.

Either already at the end of the 13th or in the 1st half of the 14th century the castle grounds were reduced in size and surrounded by a **new curtain wall**. In the process the existing buildings in the north-west (*palas*, small round tower and maybe *Holzstube* as well) were integrated into the northern curtain wall. **(fig. 12)** This is why the small round tower near the *palas* protrudes from the curtain wall, since when it was constructed in the 13th century, it did not stand at the edge of the cliff but on the originally much wider plateau. After the inner surface of the castle was diminished, the high medieval fortification elements such as the curtain wall, gate and most likely also the ditch were demolished or filled in. In the north the **outer ward (7)** was created, and together with it the **third castle gate (16)**. It was almost certainly located near the present gate. The outer ward wall run along the northern edge of the plateau, parallel to the curtain wall. It connected to the curtain wall in the east and ended in the west with a gate – the 'outer' castle gate. At the same time the entrance to the castle grounds was moved to the west. Parts of the outer ward wall are still preserved in the north-west.

Concurrent with the reduction of the living area and steepening of the escarpments, a wall-ditch system was created, surrounding the grounds in the south, west and east and adjoining the outer ward in the north. The ditch running along the eastern side of the castle with its accompanying wall could have been created as early as the High Middle Ages.

In the course of the 14th century, due to the insecure political situation the castle was considered liable to attacks and was manned by so called *Burgmannen*, sources mentioning up to 15 of those. *Burgmann* was a position with duties similar to that of a steward or a warden, responsible also for defending the castle if needed. This is how the numerous *Burgmannensitze* (also known as **Kemenaten**) – a kind of garrison – were created to accommodate the growing crew **(8 and 9)**. Two of them have been preserved until today in the northern part of the castle. The whole inner area along the curtain wall was completely remodelled probably in connection to the building of those *Burgmannensitze*.

During the 15th century aside from remodelling of the *palas*, building of the well house and some alterations to the gate house, no large-scale new developments took place. The excavations have proven that in the 15th century the 1st late medieval *palas* **(Palas I)** was partially destroyed by fire and its southern and eastern walls were altered. For the new palas **(Palas II)** an **arcade** opening to the courtyard was created in the east. At the same time the 13th century small round tower was demolished and its foundations were integrated into the residential building, most likely to create a kitchen area, and covered with a vaulted ceiling. The building that came into being had the length of c. 25 m and the width of 10 to 11 m. An 1803 graphic shows the northern aspect of the 15th century ruined *palas* with the arcades surrounding the courtyard. In the background we can see the fragment of the round tower incorporated into the residential building. **(fig. 13)**

South of the preserved Kemenate, another building with a cellar was built – the **Kemenate of the von Trott family (9)**. For this construction the **gate complex (11)** had been redesigned. It now ran from the chapel tower to the southwest corner of the Trott house. The hole for the draw bolt is still recognisable there.

At the end of the 15th century and the beginning of the 16th century (1489, 1516) almost the entire curtain wall underwent an extensive restoration and the present-day gate **(17; fourth gate)** was inserted into it. Its creation dates back to 1500.

After the heavy damages of the Great Peasants' War of 1525, since 1576 several demolition works were conducted in the keep. Afterwards the complex gradually fell into disrepair. In 1784 Duke Georg I of Sachsen-Meiningen ordered plans to be drawn to construct a folly in the bailey. The first detailed depiction of the castle ruin was the unprinted work of Christian Juncker *Ehre der gefürsteten Grafschaft Henneberg* (*Glory of the Princely Countship of Henneberg*) from 1703. (**fig. 14**) It shows the entire castle complex viewed from the west at the beginning of the 18th century. In the 19th century not only the full view of the castle hill but also the inside of the castle with the ruins of the late Gothic house was eagerly depicted.

The archaeological finds

The finds date to the Hallstatt period, the Middle Ages and the Modern Era. The Hallstatt period finds consist mainly of pottery shards (c. 5300 pieces) and small finds. Among them, there are a funnel and two spindle whorls made of burned clay (**fig. 15**), an arm bracelet, two tubes and an axe made of bronze. Worth noticing is a well-preserved amber bead. (**fig. 16**) It is highly probable that the bead was not made locally but imported to Henneburg.

More than 16.400 medieval pottery shards were found. Some with early lead glaze deserve special attention. They are dated between the 11th and early 13th century. Another interesting find is a red piece of thrown pottery, probably manufactured in Mayen, district Koblenz-Mayen, dating to the late 12th – early 13th century. According to the recent studies Henneberg was the south-eastern distribution point for this type of pottery. In the late 12th till the early 14th century pots made of rough, white clay were also in use in the Henneberg castle. Of one of such pots only the bottom part, painted red-brown, remained. It is unique amongst the Henneberg finds. (**fig. 17**) Smaller medieval clay objects include fragments of small sculptures, gaming pieces, marbles, spindle whorls and loom weights.

Among iron objects there are tools such as knives, sheers, drills, sickles, a file, an axe and a hoe. Parts of a mounted lock, keys, door hinges, nails, bolts, hooks and fittings as well as a candlestick stem from the domestic area. Arrow heads appear in various shapes and sizes. Snuffle bits, spurs, a stirrup, a curry comb, saddle buckles, horseshoes and horseshoe nails belong to the equestrian equipment. A caltrop and an iron jaw harp (**fig. 18**) are unique.

Two knife sheaths fittings are made of iron and bronze. Clothing accessories such as buckles of iron or bronze or brass are rare. Finds of objects made of non-ferrous metals include rings and earrings, chains, pendants, clasps, buttons and modern coins. (fig. 19) Medieval coins were not recorded. However, it is reported that in 1832 Johann Philipp Heinrich Hartmann found a whole roll of silver coins.

Worth mentioning is a rhombic ornamented brass fitting dating to the 10th–11th century. (fig. 20) Another find of particular interest is a brass seal ring, with the initials M v H set in a shield shape. (fig. 21) This ring could have belonged to Mathes von Hönningen, who was one of the *Burgmannen* of Henneburg and died in 1576. Worth paying attention to is also a gilded bronze pendant depicting a hen. (fig. 22) This find originates from a feature dating to the 12th- early 13th century. What makes it so noteworthy is its connection to the House of Henneberg, whose coat of arms depicts a hen! The pendant would have been worn during the reign of Poppo VII and his wife Jutta. The gilding clearly points to the high status of the owner.

Numerous fragments of bronze sheet, a bronze lid and a bronze 3-legged pot represent the cookware. A bronze bell and a pointed object of unknown purpose complement the inventory of non-ferrous finds. Glass shards are fragments of glass containers and glass panes. There is also a remarkably large number of glass rings. (fig. 23) They are otherwise relatively rare in Thuringian castles. The presence of so many rings, as well as other glass objects, indicate a presence of a glass workshop near Henneberg.

Amongst the surface finds from the southern part of the excavation area there is a yellowish-red sandstone ashlar with a chessboard pattern. (fig. 24) Stones with a chessboard pattern were a widespread motif since the early 12th century used solely in sacral buildings. There are numerous examples of such features in Romanesque Benedictine and Premonstratensian monastery churches. They can also be seen in the Henneberg family monastery in Veßra, district Hildburghausen, founded in 1131 by Gotebold of Henneberg.

Amongst the ample collection of the animal bones there are also objects manufactured of bones and antler such as dice, combs, decorative panels, gaming pieces, a bead and a button. (fig. 25)

The entire bone material underwent archaeozoological investigation. This material is perfectly suited to reconstruct the eating habits of the people inhabiting the castle. It shows the correlation between the choice and the age of the animals at the moment of slaughter or culling as well as the preference of certain body parts of particular domestic and wild animals and the quality of the meat-based diet. The vast majority of the animal bones come from pigs (c. 2/3). Sheep or goats (c.1/4) and cattle were decisively less often consumed. Following domestic animals were present at the castle: horse, donkey, cat, dog, chicken and goose. Wild animals and fish constitute a minor share. Red deer, boar, hare, brown bear, beaver, black grouse and herring could be accounted for. A talon of an eagle was found as well.

Animals with relatively high-quality meat predominate in the castle. In comparison to the other medieval Thuringian castles, in the High and also Late Middle Ages Henneburg takes the top position in the consumption of high quality nourishment, ranking even higher than Wartburg near Eisenach. This result implies that during the Middle Ages the castle was inhabited by a group of people of a higher social status and, therefore, more economically secured.

Tour

The mighty silhouette of the tower and the extensive grounds enclosed by the curtain wall constitute the best preserved parts. Next to them, in the north stands a small residential building and south of it the remains of another building with a cellar. The residual, formerly very substantial collection of buildings is partially revealed through the excavations and visible as foundation walls and partially recorded in old depictions as well as recognisable through manifold traces in the curtain wall. **(fig. 26)** The **curtain wall** has the total length of about 300 m and remains in some places more than 10 m high. The varying wall thickness of 0.75 to 1.25 m, as well as diverse mortar joints, building joints and presence of reclaimed stones indicate a multi-phased construction process. With the exception of a longer segment in the north-west, dating from the 13th century, the curtain wall seems to have been extensively remade in the Late Middle Ages. Between 1991 and 2002 substantial restoration work on the wall took place. On the upper parts of the curtain wall one still can distinguish numerous traces of buildings previously abutting its inner side. Beam holes, putlog holes and horizontal recesses indicating the previously existing storeys, wall stubs or traces of transverse walls, windows and embrasures, garderobes and chimneys point to the high number of *Burgmannsitzen*, 15 of which were mentioned during the 14th century. It seems that buildings were put up alongside almost the entire length of the curtain wall. A great number of late medieval buildings bordering the wall are marked on the plan created by Ernst Abesser between 1880 and 1883. **(see fig. 3)** Precise dating of all segments of the wall borders are impossible since the datable elements are missing almost completely and the joints have been repointed multiple times since 1990 through the various restoration campaigns.

Today, one enters the castle grounds through a **gate (17)** located in the north-east. **(fig. 27)** It was erected about 1500 and is subsequently the fourth one. The first gate existed in the High Middle Ages in the south of the castle complex, the second (the pincer gate) in the northeast of the palace. In the 13th century it was replaced by gate no. 3 **(16)** about 10 m north of the present entrance. The latter was inserted between two older sections of the curtain wall. To the outside it is not flash with the wall but set back a bit. On the courtyard side, the two upper pivot stones of the gate wings are still preserved. The two cheek walls running inwards indicate a small gate tower. They exhibit distinct traces of burning, which are probably connected with the storming of the castle in the Peasants' War of 1525. The ditch located in front of the gate was filled in order to create a ramp leading to the castle. About 1700 a pillar from the bridge previously traversing the ditch was still extant.

Exactly opposite there are the imposing remains of the keep **(Tower II; 18)**, measuring 14 metres in diameter. Its ground floor is accessible through a gap created in the 18th century in the north-east side. It is vaulted by a 10 m high dome made of stone slabs. At its apex there is a circular opening which was originally the only access to the basement. **(fig. 28)** The dating of the tower to the middle till the 2nd half of the 13th century is possible due to the comparatively sloppy quality of its masonry, consisting not, as the other towers of the castles belonging to the Hennebergs, of ashlars but of rubble masonry. Additionally the irregularity and unevenness of the mortar joints stand out. In 1885 the tower was remodelled into a lookout tower and for that purpose a cast iron staircase was added. In 2000 the dilapidated 19th century stairs were removed and replaced by a modern construction similar in form.

Approximately in the middle of the northern curtain wall a two-storey square residential building (8; *Kemenate*) rises, which can be perceived as living quarters for one of the numerous *Burgmannen*. A small arched or double arch window is located in the northern part of the ground floor. (fig. 29) The window is not a part of the original structure but was probably moved there in the 19th century as can be substantiated by the broken reveal, the damage around it and the unquestionably late medieval masonry surrounding the window.

The well (4) located in the north was, in all probability, also created in the High Middle Ages. The well shaft, cut into the muschelkalk bedrock, has a diameter of 2.50 m. Its upper part is lined with roughly worked stones. In 1996 the well was excavated to a depth of 12.80 m but its total depth could not be determined. There is evidence of a well house dating back to the Late Middle Ages. South of the *Kemenate* there are remains of a second *Kemenate* (9) with the entrance to the cellar still preserved. It dates from the late 14th/15th century and was the residence of the von Trott Burgmann family. On its south-west wall the hole for the draw bolt of the rebuilt courtyard gate can still be seen. (fig. 30)

Several significant remains of the residential building in the north-west of the castle complex have been preserved. Most striking is a large arch of shell limestone ashlars in the curtain wall, spanning about eight metres and visible from the outside as well as from the inside. (fig. 31) Underneath the arch there are three rows of partially walled up window openings in the following arrangement: two in row above, three in the middle row and four in the bottom; their layout roughly forms a triangle. These are the remains of a *Holzstube* (14). The function of a *Holzstube* was heat retention. In order to prevent the warmth from escaping to the outside, the windows were small, but numerous. The Henneberg *Holzstube* was probably heated with movable heat sources such as heat trays. There is no evidence of underfloor heating or a tiled stove. A wooden window frame remained in place until 1992. It was made of fir wood and could be dated to 1295–1305. (**fig. 32**) This makes the Henneberg *Holzstube* one of the oldest in the castles of the German-speaking area.

Burn marks on the inner surface of the wall are evidence of a fire which engulfed the ground and upper floors. The *Holzstube* was demolished in the late Middle Ages. The windows in the upper and lower row were added and five corbels rounded off at the front were inserted. Two middle corbels sit in the window openings of the upper row. The southernmost corbel is intersected by a transverse wall and, thus, testifies to its later origin. The small rectangular window to the north of the arch was inserted in the 19th century to close a gap in the wall.

Another important feature concerns the only partially preserved upper floor of the *Holzstube*. Its western wall was decorated with an unusually elaborate row of windows overlooking the landscape whose characteristic shapes are well known due to numerous depictions (first by Christian Juncker 1703, see **fig. 14**). The row of four identical sandstone windows, their upper parts shaped like three-leaf clover, continued to be depicted in numerous artworks throughout the 19th century. (**fig. 33**) Due to their elaborate shape it can be expected that the windows illuminated some opulently furnished living quarters. From the whole row only the reveal of the southern window remained.

East of the *Holzstube*, the foundation walls of the choir added in the 14th century to the 13th-century **chapel tower (15)** and of the adjoining trapezoidal building (**12; Building IX**) are still visible. The **round tower**, located further direction north, is a 13th century addition to the *palas*. Its current appearance dates from the end of the 19th century. When the residential building (**1; palas**) was extended to the south and east at the end of the 14th century, the round tower was partially demolished and the remaining half was vaulted over. The new building was given an upper storey, the south wall of which today reaches the same height as the lower of the viewing platform. (**fig. 34**) The building faced west with two two-light rectangular windows; only a fragment of the jamb at the north end of the wall has survived from a third window. The old chimney was raised to create a fireplace on the upper floor and is still visible on the outside of the wall. (see fig. 9) The late Gothic residential building burnt out during the Peasants' War in 1525, as indicated by burn marks on the ground and upper floor of the west wall.

Approximately in the **middle of the western side** the curtain wall suddenly bends at a straight angle only to bend again after 4.5 m and follow further direction north. Here, in the 14th century, stood a building, whose eastern, southern and western walls are still extant. Nowadays the niche is filled in by a new construction added in 1996. The adjoining section of the wall, of which two storeys remain today, dates from around 1300. (fig. 35) The opening on the ground floor, which served as an entrance to a garderobe, is flanked by a slit window and a small rectangular window. On the upper floor a double lancet window suggests a living area. The jambs outside have holes for fixing shutters. Directly south of the window, a niche, which can be interpreted as a closet, is cut out in the wall. The inner surface of the wall shows traces of burning.

Remains of the inner buildings are also preserved at the **southern section of the curtain wall**. (fig. 36) A ledge and some putlog holes mark the level where the ceiling of the cellar previously was. The cellar was ventilated through two slit windows still visible from the outside. The larger window was a part of the ground floor. East of it one can still spot remains of a demolished transverse wall which originally closed off the building to the east, while west of it there is a slit window and a candle niche. They are followed by a walled up garderobe, whose northern reveal is aligned with a second transverse wall, and two more slit windows. The lower part of yet another window and two corbels of the chimney hood point to the existance of an upper floor. The section of wall described above is probably connected with two renovations of the curtain wall in recorded 1489 and 1516.

The bulge in the course of the wall in the southeast is the result of the renovation of the wall in 2001/2002 when the high medieval round tower (19; Tower I) was reconstructed as a semicircle, clearly visible on the outside. (Fig. 37) In 1845 part of the southern section of the western wall were underpinned by two pillars connected with an arch.

Today, only a few beam holes, window openings and garderobes remain as evidence of the original interior construction in the **east of the castle complex**. Numerous reclaimed stones were set into the eastern part of the curtain wall. Among them, there are three stones on the outside, decorated with hemispheres which used to belong to an arched window in the late Romanesque residential building. **(fig. 38)** Similar arched windows with this kind of hemisphere decoration can be found in the Town Square Apothecary in Saalfeld, district Saalfeld-Rudolstadt.

A little further south, three garderobes can be identified, two of which are walled up. The remains of the corbels which used to support them are still clearly visible on the outside. **(fig. 39)** This wall section probably dates to the 14th/15th century.

Due to its location on the former inner-German border, Henneberg Castle was somewhat forgotten in the last decades of the 20th century. That changed with the German reunification in 1989. Archaeological excavations and the work of historians and building researchers in the 1990s to 2002 have enormously increased our knowledge of this important castle complex. The late medieval curtain wall, the mighty keep or the *Holzstube*, which is one of the oldest buildings of its kind in the German-speaking world, still bear witness to the power of the Henneberg counts. In the High and Late Middle Ages, they not only shaped the history of southern Thuringia and Lower Franconia, but also played a prominent role in the history of the Holy Roman Empire under count Berthold VII.

Tasks and goals

The ruins of Henneberg Castle are one of the most important testimonies to a long-gone dynasty, the Counts of Henneberg. As is often the case with abandoned sites, only parts of the former castle have survived and of the original buildings, only a few walls remain. The most visible features are the remnants of the keep, which the Palace, Castle and Gardens Trust of Thuringia made accessible again over 20 years ago, as well as the curtain wall, parts of the Kemenate, remains of the chapel and the small round tower. The archaeological excavations carried out by the Thuringian State Office for the Preservation of Historical Monuments during the renovation contributed significantly to our understanding of the development of the castle complex throughout centuries.

The castle is open to the public and is an important stop for hikers on their way through the Grabfeld region and along the national "Green Belt" trail. In order to highlight the historical significance of the site for southern Thuringia and northern Lower Franconia, the results of the archaeological investigations are going to be presented on the castle grounds, thus giving visitors a better understanding of the former importance of the ancestral castle of the counts of Henneberg.

This project will be realised in cooperation with the Thuringian State Office for the Preservation of Monuments and Archaeology.

Since 1995 the Trust has looked after the Henneberg castle as a part of its ruin preservation scheme. Its condition is regularily examined and, when necessary, restoration work is carried out. To maintain its status as a focal point for the region, a strict program of vegetation management will be introduced around the castle grounds.

The castle ruins are looked after on a voluntary basis by the Club Henneberg e. V., which was founded in 1990. The organisation takes care of the ongoing maintenance of the grounds and offers events, including the biennial castle festival, but is also the on-site contact for visitors and serves as the castle administration on behalf of the the Palace, Castle and Gardens Trust of Thuringia.

Chronology

7th/6th century BC	A first fortification was constructed on the 'Schlossberg' (Castle Hill)
2nd half of the 10th century	The first castle was founded by the Counts of Schweinfurt on the northern edge of their dominion; the buildings I–III, IV (residential tower), V and VI date from this period also presumably the well
about 1000/1030	The first Round Tower in the south of the castle and the first curtain wall were erected, a gate was presumably located in the south of the castle complex
1096	The first mentioning of the Henneberg family (Gotebold II)
1190	The house was divided into the line of Henneberg and the collateral lines of Botenlauben and Strauf
about 1200	The first Round Tower was dismantled and the entrance to the castle was moved to the north-west (pincer gate = the second gate)
1221	The first direct documented reference to the Henneberg Castle as 'castrum'
1st half of the 13th century	Under Poppo VII (died in 1245) and his wife Jutta major alterations take place. The Palas I, a small round tower and a new courtyard gateway in the north-west of the castle are build and a chaple is installed in the tower house
after 1245	Poppo's son Berthold from his first marriage inherits the ancestral castle and most of his father's property; under his son Hermann from his second marriage the "New Lordship of Henneberg" came into being
1253	The presence of a chaplain is first mentioned

around 1250	Construction of the keep
1274	The house is divided into the lines of Schleusingen, Aschach and Hartenberg. The Henneburg passed into the hands of Berthold V (†1284)
13th century	Major alterations took place in the castle. The first curtain wall was dismantled and the castle grounds were reduced in size. A new curtain wall was erected integrating the existing palas, the round tower and the *Holzstube*. In the north the outer ward was created, and together with it the third castle gate. It was located near the present day entrance
about 1300	The *Holzstube* was build
End of the 13th/ beginning of the 14th century	Under Berthold VII (died in 1340) the family seat was moved to Schleusingen. The castle was remodelled into a military stronghold
1308	A lightning stroke damaged one of the large towers to collapse (the chapel tower or the small round tower?). Afterwards the southern wall of the palas was remodelled to integrate the foundation of the tower. At the same time the trapezoid building (building IX) was erected
around 1330	Sources are mentioning 15 so called Burgmannen which held duties similar to that of a steward or a warden. This shows the insecure political situation of the castle
1393	A part of the castle was given to Friedrich I of the Henneberg-Römhild line by his father in law count Heinrich X of Henneberg-Schleusingen as a dowry
1432	The castle was divided between the sons of Heinrich X and Friedrich I
15th century	The palas was partially destroyed by fire and its southern and eastern walls were altered. An arcade opening to the courtyard was created in the east. The upper floor contained a fireplace.

Three rectangular windows illuminated the room. The well house and a Kemenate for the von Trott family was build. The gate house was remodelled

1489 and 1516	Comprehensive renovation of the curtain wall. The Castle gate was moved to its present day position (fourth gate)
1525	The castle was severly damaged during the Peasants' War
Middle of the 16th century	First demolition work on the castle and especially on the keep to extract building materials
End of the 16th century	Burkhard Herman von Trott ist the last Burgmann living in the castle
18th century	An entrance is created in the ground floor of the keep
1784	Duke Georg I of Sachsen-Meiningen orders the bailey to be leveled
from 1843	First restoration works are carried out by master builder August Wilhelm Döbner
1879–1883	First excavation and further conservation works by Ernst Abesser. A first site plan was drawn
around 1935	Excavations by Friedrich Tenner
1992–1995	Four excavation campaigns in the northwestern castle grounds and reconstruction of the unearthed foundation walls
2001/2002	Restoration of the south-east curtain wall. During the archeological survey the foundation of the high medieval round tower was discoverd. It was replicated in shape of a semicircle incorporated into the curtain wall in the south

Weiterführende Literatur | Further Reading

Bartel, Kevin 2010: Henneburg und Heldburg – Zwei ältereisenzeitliche Höhensiedlungen in Südthüringen, unveröff. Magisterarbeit.

Dehio, Georg: Handbuch der Deutschen Kunstdenkmäler, Thüringen, bearb. von Stephanie Eißing u. a., München/Berlin 1998.

Küchenmeister, Ralf: Ausgrabungen auf der Burg „Henneburg", Lkr. Schmalkalden-Meiningen, in: Ausgrabungen und Funde im Freistaat Thüringen, Bd. 6, 2002, S. 35–43.

Mötsch, Johannes: Regesten des Archivs der Grafen von Henneberg-Römhild (Veröffentlichungen der Historischen Kommission für Thüringen, Große Reihe 13), Köln/ Weimar/Wien 2006.

Mötsch, Johannes; Witter, Katharina: Die ältesten Lehnsbücher der Grafen von Henneberg (Veröffentlichungen aus Thüringischen Staatsarchiven, Bd. 2), Weimar 1996.

Schwarzberg, Heiner: Ausgrabungen auf der Burg Henneberg, Lkr. Schmalkalden-Meiningen. Vorbericht, in: Ausgrabungen und Funde, Bd. 40, 1995, S. 265–272.

Schwarzberg, Heiner: Die Ausgrabungen auf der Burg Henneberg. Vorbericht der Kampagnen 1992–1995, in: Wissenschaftliche Festschrift zum Jubiläum „900 Jahre Henneberger Land 1096–1996" (Jahrbuch des Hennebergisch-Fränkischen Geschichtsvereins, Bd. 11), S. 153–168, Kloster Veßra/Meiningen/ Münnerstadt 1996.

Spazier, Ines: Die Burgruine Henneberg in Südthüringen. Stammburg der Henneberger Grafen (Weimarer Monographien zur Ur- und Frühgeschichte, Bd. 44), Langenweißbach 2017.

Spazier, Ines; Schwarzberg, Heiner: Die Burg Henneberg/Südthüringen im 11. und 12. Jahrhundert. In: Neue Forschungen zum frühen Burgenbau. Jahrestagung der Wartburg-Gesellschaft vom 3. bis 6. April 2003 in Quedlinburg (Forschung zu Burgen und Schlössern, Bd. 9), S. 187–204. München, Berlin 2006.

Tenner, Friedrich: Burg Henneberg. Der Stammsitz des Hennebergischen Grafenhauses. Meiningen (Volkstümliche Schriftenreihe des Hennebergisch-Fränkischen Geschichtsvereins, H. 1), Meiningen [1936], Nachdruck Neustadt a. d. Aisch 1996.

Wagner, Heinrich: Zur urkundlichen Erstnennung des Namens Henneberg, in: Wissenschaftliche Festschrift zum Jubiläum „900 Jahre Henneberger Land 1096–1996" (Jahrbuch des Hennebergisch-Fränkischen Geschichtsvereins, Bd. 11), S. 25–32, Kloster Veßra/Meiningen/Münnerstadt 1996.

Wagner, Heinrich: Entwurf einer Genealogie der Grafen von Henneberg, in: Wissenschaftliche Festschrift zum Jubiläum „900 Jahre Henneberger Land 1096–1996" (Jahrbuch des Hennebergisch-Fränkischen Geschichtsvereins, Bd. 11), S. 33–152, Kloster Veßra/Meiningen/Münnerstadt 1996.

Wojaczek, Christoph: Die Burg Henneberg, in: Südliches Thüringen (Führer zu archäologischen Denkmälern in Deutschland, Bd. 28 = Archäologische Denkmale in Thüringen, Bd. 1), S. 222–227, Stuttgart 1994.

Zeune, Joachim: Kleinfenstergruppen und Trichterfenster an mittelalterlichen Burgen, in: Barbara Schock-Werner (Hrsg.): Fenster und Türen in historischen Wehr- und Wohnbauten. Kolloquium des Wissenschaftlichen Beirats der Deutschen Burgenvereinigung (Veröffentlichungen der Deutschen Burgenvereinigung e. V., Bd. 4), S. 51–60, Stuttgart 1995.

Abbildungsnachweis | Photo Credits

Abb. 1: Thomas Spazier (TLDA, Weimar)

Abb. 2, 12: Martin Milbradt (TLDA, Weimar)

Abb. 3: LATh – StA Meiningen, Staatliches Hochbauamt Hildburghausen, Mappe 25, Blatt 2

Abb. 4, 5, 8, 9, 10, 11, 12, 27, 29, 32, 34, 38: TLDA, Weimar, Fotodokumentation Henneberg

Abb. 6, 15, 16, 20, 21, 23, 25: Hauke Arnold (TLDA, Weimar)

Abb. 7, 31, 35, 37, 39: Ines Spazier (TLDA, Weimar)

Abb. 12: Steffen Ittig, proofpic.gbr

Abb. 13: Meininger Museen

Abb. 14: LATh-StA Meiningen, Henneberg aus Gotha, Nr. 369

Abb. 17, 18, 19, 22, 24: Brigitte Stefan (TLDA, Weimar)

Abb. 28, 36: Benjamin Rudolph (Weimar)

Abb. 30: Grit Heßland (Rittersdorf)

Abb. 33: LATh-StA Gotha, Geheimes Archiv, 00 I, Nr. 47-1

Umschlagplan: Plan Büro Langlotz (Vacha). Bearbeitung Ines und Thomas Spazier (TLDA, Weimar)

Titelbild: Martin Milbradt (TLDA, Weimar)

Umschlagrückseite: Grit Heßland (Rittersdorf)

Lageplan Burg Henneberg

1   Gebäude I, III, V, Palas (Wohngebäude), teils in der Ringmauer erhalten / Building I, III, V, *palas*

2   Gebäude VI (quadratischer Bau) / Building VI

3   zweites Burgtor (Zangentor) / second castle gate (pincer gate)

4   Brunnen (erhalten) / well

5   Gebäude VIII (Torturm) / Building VIII (gate tower)

6   Gebäude II (Wohnbau, Fachwerk) / Building II

7   Zwinger mit „äußerem Burgtor" im Westen / outer ward with gate in the west

8   Ruine einer Kemenate (erhalten) / *Kemenate*

9   Ruine der Trott'schen Kemenate (erhalten) / *Kemenate* of the von Trott family

10 erste Hoftoranlage / first gate complex

11 zweite Hoftoranlage /second gate complex

12 Gebäude IX (trapezförmiges Gebäude) / Building IX (trapezoidal building)

13 kleiner Rundturm beim Palas (wiederaufgebaut) / small round tower (rebuilt)

14 Gebäude VII (Holz- oder Bohlenstube, teils in der Ringmauer erhalten) / Building VII (*Holzstube*)

15 Gebäude IV (Wohnturm, Kapellenturm, Kapelle, teils erhalten) / Building IV (tower house, chapel tower, chapel)

16 drittes Burgtor (teils in der Ringmauer erhalten) / third gate

17 viertes Burgtor / forth castle gate

18 Bergfried 2 (erhalten) / keep (Tower II)

19 Bergfried 1 / round tower (Tower I)

20 erstes Burgtor / first castle gate

21 Steinbearbeitungsgrube / building area

22 Gebäude X (Mauerreste) / Building X

(Die im Text fett gedruckten Nummern entsprechen denen in der Karte.)